Management Extra

FINANCIAL MANAGEMENT

T0382935

Management Extra

FINANCIAL MANAGEMENT

Pergamon
Flexible
Learning

AMSTERDAM • BOSTON • HEIDELBERG • LONDON • NEW YORK • OXFORD • PARIS •
SAN DIEGO • SAN FRANCISCO • SINGAPORE • SYDNEY • TOKYO

Pergamon Flexible Learning is an imprint of Elsevier
Linacre House, Jordan Hill, Oxford OX2 8DP, UK
30 Corporate Drive, Suite 400, Burlington, MA 01803, USA

First published 2005
Revised edition 2008

Notice
No responsibility is assumed by the publisher for any injury and/or damage
to persons or property as a matter of products liability, negligence or
otherwise, or from any use or operation of any methods, products,
instructions or ideas contained in the material herein.

British Library Cataloguing in Publication Data
A catalogue record for this book is available from the British Library

Library of Congress Cataloging-in-Publication Data
A catalog record for this book is available from the Library of Congress

ISBN 978-0-08-055235-4

For information on all Pergamon Flexible Learning publications visit
our web site at www.books.elsevier.com

Printed and bound in Italy

Contents

Activities

Figures

Tables

Series preface

Whether you are a tutor/trainer or studying management development to further your career, Management Extra provides an exciting and flexible resource helping you to achieve your goals. The series is completely new and up-to-date, and has been written to harmonise with the 2004 national occupational standards in management and leadership. It has also been mapped to management qualifications, including the Institute of Leadership & Management's middle and senior management qualifications at Levels 5 and 7 respectively on the revised national framework.

For learners, coping with all the pressures of today's world, Management Extra offers you the flexibility to study at your own pace to fit around your professional and other commitments. Suddenly, you don't need a PC or to attend classes at a specific time – choose when and where to study to suit yourself! And, you will always have the complete workbook as a quick reference just when you need it.

For tutors/trainers, Management Extra provides an invaluable guide to what needs to be covered, and in what depth. It also allows learners who miss occasional sessions to 'catch up' by dipping into the series.

This series provides unrivalled support for all those involved in management development at middle and senior levels.

Reviews of Management Extra

I have utilised the Management Extra series for a number of Institute of Leadership and Management (ILM) Diploma in Management programmes. The series provides course tutors with the flexibility to run programmes in a variety of formats, from fully facilitated, using a choice of the titles as supporting information, to a tutorial based programme, where the complete series is provided for home study. These options also give course participants the flexibility to study in a manner which suits their personal circumstances. The content is interesting, thought provoking and up-to-date, and, as such, I would highly recommend the use of this series to suit a variety of individual and business needs.

Martin Davies BSc(Hons) MEd CEngMIMechE MCIPD FITOL FInstLM
Senior Lecturer, University of Wolverhampton Business School

At last, the complete set of books that make it all so clear and easy to follow for tutor and student. A must for all those taking middle/senior management training seriously.

Michael Crothers, ILM National Manager

Why financial management matters

We all need to be financial managers in our daily lives: we need to match our expenditure with income, arrange a loan where there is a temporary shortfall in funds and invest money to make our future more secure.

As money plays an important role in our private lives, so it does in the management of organisations. Commercial organisations exist primarily to make money.

'Annual income twenty pounds, annual expenditure nineteen, nineteen six, result happiness. Annual income twenty pounds, annual expenditure twenty pounds ought and six, result misery' – Mr Micawber in *David Copperfield*, Charles Dickens (1849–1850).

At work, non-specialists are sometimes reluctant to get involved in the finances of their organisations, but effective financial management is so central to success that it requires input from everyone within the organisation.

'Your specialist skills are a barrier not a route to success.' This advice to a young accountant starting his first job in industry perhaps holds a message for everyone. What it is saying is that managers can find a false security in their own specialisation, whether it lies in finance, production, marketing, human resources or research.

In today's fast-moving environment, this is clearly a recipe for disaster. To gain competitive advantage, all parts of an organisation must be able to talk to one another. It follows then that all managers must be, in some sense, financial managers who are able to speak the common language of finance.

This module aims to provide you with the necessary understanding to input into the financial management of your organisation.

> The financial management attributes of organisations are no longer the prerogative and sole responsibility of higher echelons of management, but are now the day-to-day currency of all managers.
>
> **Broadbent and Cullen (2003)**

Your objectives during this module are to:
- Be able to contribute more effectively to the financial planning process in your organisation
- Investigate the relationship between costing and pricing of products
- Learn to prepare capital investment proposals
- Use the main financial statements and key financial ratios to evaluate an organisation's performance
- Identify the main sources of funding for an organisation.

Important note on this book

The examples used throughout the book are drawn from profit-making organisations but are relevant to other forms of enterprise. Public and not-for-profit organisations also have a duty to manage their money efficiently and effectively so as to meet their objectives and further the aims of their stakeholders. Nearly everything covered in this book applies to these organisations, either directly or because they have trading activities that help them to achieve their aims.

1 Key financial statements

Your company is preparing a plan to increase profits by 10 per cent next year. *What do all managers need to understand before they can start to contribute to the plan?*

All managers with collective responsibility for preparing and then implementing the plan need to understand:

◆ What is meant by the term 'profit'

◆ How they are expected to contribute to the financial plan

◆ How their own actions will impact upon the financial measures

◆ The way in which changes in the business environment, for example, a downturn in the economy will impact upon the actions necessary to achieve the financial plan.

> **A company without cash cannot buy the people, materials or equipment it needs and without these a profit cannot be earned.**
>
> **Owen**
> **(2003)**

In this theme you will start to develop your understanding of financial matters by investigating the main statements used to present financial information. All financial reports aim to 'tell a story' about how a business is performing. The financial statements tell you about past performance or plans of an organisation, and help you to make decisions about the direction of the business.

Throughout the book we ask you to relate what you learn to the practice within your organisation, and to ask questions which perhaps you have felt reluctant to ask in the past.

In this theme, you will:

◆ **Explore why cash planning is essential to running a business and practise preparing a cash flow forecast**

◆ **Discover how profit measurement differs from cash flow and why both profit and cash are essential indicators of business performance**

◆ **Practise preparing a profit and loss account forecast**

◆ **Learn about the main types of assets in a business**

◆ **Prepare a simple forecast balance sheet.**

Activity 1
Financial reporting

Objective

This first activity asks you to gather some information about the financial management of your own organisation, business unit or department.

Task

Ask what information is available about the financial management of your own department or business unit. Find out what:

◆ financial responsibilities different people hold

◆ reports are produced to control expenditure

◆ other reports are produced to monitor the performance of the department or business unit.

Make notes in the charts provided about the different responsibilities and financial reports. You will be returning to your own organisation's reporting in later activities, so consider this activity as the first stage of a continuing process.

Financial responsibilities

Name	Job Title	Responsibilities

Expenditure reports

Name	When produced (weekly, monthly, etc.)	Purpose and description

Other reports		
Name	*When produced (weekly, monthly, etc.)*	*Purpose and description*

Feedback

Don't worry if you have obtained only limited information at this stage. As you progress through this book you will be able to be more specific about the information you would like to see and so more likely to obtain examples from your workplace.

You may have been told that certain information is confidential. This is fine, just relate the information in the book as far as you are able to what happens at your workplace.

You can also relate the information in this book to the management of your own family finances. The financial management of the cash flow into and, more difficult, out of our bank accounts is something for which we all have to take responsibility.

In addition, most people have thought about starting a new business venture at some time or you may know somebody who is in business on their own. You may find it very informative to produce some of the example forecasts and statements in the text for your own business idea or to apply them to a friend's business.

Finally, as you work through the different sections, if you do not understand something on the information you have obtained, then ask your manager, colleagues or the finance specialists. This should present an excellent opportunity to expand your knowledge.

Cash is king

You may have heard the expression 'the bottom line', which originates from the last line of a financial statement that shows the profit for the year. In general usage, the bottom line is the end result by which the plan and the people responsible for that plan will be judged. For example, in a political election there may be all sorts of considerations, but for political activists the bottom line is whether or not their party gets elected.

Considering the origin of the expression, it is perhaps strange that for a business the true bottom line is not profit but cash. We will look at profit in the next section but first we will consider why cash is king.

Cash and cash flow

When we talk about 'cash' or 'cash flow' we are not using the words in any specialist sense. If you have more money in your bank account at the end of the month than you started with at the beginning of the month, then you have increased the amount of cash you have available to spend and have a positive cash flow.

Similarly, if there is a payroll breakdown in your organisation and this month's salary is not paid into your bank account, then your cheques may well start to bounce. It is no good telling people the money is 'really' there; either it is there or it is not. With cash, the only reality is whether the money appears on your bank statement.

Cash flow forecasting

Angela is thinking of setting up on her own in business as an information systems consultant. She currently has a bank balance of £1,500. In order to meet her mortgage and other personal financial commitments, she must take £1,000 from the business each month. Angela thinks this should not be a problem.

She has been promised business worth £2,000 a month from the start and her business expenses will only be about £800.

At the start of each month she will invoice customers for the previous month and give them 30 days to pay. Business expenses are mainly for items like petrol and will be settled as she goes along.

Is Angela right when she says she does not have a problem?

If Angela starts trading in January, let us simply set out the movements on her bank statement month by month – see Table 1.1.

	Start of month £	Money in £	Money out £	Close of month £
January	1,500	nil	1,800	(300)
February	(300)	nil	1,800	(2,100)
March	(2,100)	nil	1,800	(3,900)
April	(3,900)	2,000	1,800	(3,700)
May	(3,700)	2,000	1,800	(3,500)
June	(3,500)	2,000	1,800	(3,300)

Table 1.1 *Angela's bank account transactions*

The £1,800 in the 'Money out' column is made up of the £1,000 taken out of the business by her for personal expenses plus £800 for business expenses.

Angela will bill in early February for the work done for clients in January. Her clients interpret her '30 days credit' to mean 30 days from the end of the month in which the invoice was raised. This takes us to the last day of March. As clients always take a few more days to pay, the money for the work carried out in January will not arrive until early April.

There is clearly no future in Angela saying she is 'really' earning £2,000 a month; the reality is that she is going to have a bank overdraft of £3,900 at the end of March – which she needs to have agreed with her bank manager in advance.

Notice too how slowly the bank overdraft goes down after the end of March. It only reduces by the £200 a month her income exceeds her outgoings.

Evaluating the cash flow forecast

You are sitting down with Angela, looking at these projected overdrafts. Angela thinks she will not go self employed after all.

How would you advise her?

Hers may well be the right decision. Perhaps Angela is the sort of person who dislikes going into debt and who would be happier by staying an employee after all. Perhaps, however, she is confident that once she becomes known, she will be billing much more than £2,000 a month and is willing to present a case to the bank manager for an overdraft. It would help a great deal if she could negotiate shorter payment periods with her customers.

For Angela and for your own organisation, there is no question here of the financial analysis telling us what is the 'right' answer. Angela's decisions will depend on what she sees as the future for the business over the longer term. Nor is it just about the money; whether she goes ahead will also depend, for instance, on whether she would enjoy working on her own.

Similarly for a business, the role of financial analysis is to inform, so that the organisation can make better decisions. For example, a particular project may yield good cash flows that meet all the financial requirements by which projects are judged. Yet senior management may reject the project on the grounds that it does not fit the organisation's strategy, fearing that it would divert management resources away from the primary goals of the business.

Successful entrepreneurs with little theoretical financial understanding are mostly excellent at cash flow planning. They simply have to be. They know the staff must be paid on Friday and that unless they get the money in from last week's delivery to an important customer, they will exceed their overdraft limit.

This focus on cash generation is just as important in large corporations, but much more difficult to achieve where numerous people may take decisions which have implications for the cash flow.

> Angela negotiates with her customers to have 50 per cent payment in the month in which she works and 50 per cent the month after. She is seeing her bank manager in the morning.
>
> *What would you advise?*

The new payment terms will greatly improve Angela's cash position. Her revised forecast is shown in Table 1.2.

	Start of month £	Money in £	Money out £	Close of month £
January	1,500	1,000	1,800	700
February	700	2,000	1,800	900
March	900	2,000	1,800	1,100
April	1,100	2,000	1,800	1,300
May	1,300	2,000	1,800	1,500
June	1,500	2,000	1,800	1,700

Table 1.2 *Angela's bank account – revised forecast*

The £2,000 received in February represents £1,000 for work done in January and £1,000 for work done in February itself – and so on for each of the following months.

By advancing the cash flows into the business, Angela has avoided the need for an overdraft at all. Whilst she sees a drop in her bank balance, this has been replenished by the end of the period. This shows the importance of cash flow management to a business and why it is important not to be too generous with the amount of time you give your debtors to pay.

It may still be wise for Angela to negotiate an overdraft facility with her bank manager even if she does not ultimately need to make use of it. Even a delay of a few days in payment could lead to her needing an overdraft, especially in the first few months of trading.

Activity 2
Cash flow forecast

Objective

This activity asks you to practise preparing a cash flow forecast.

Whilst it will be possible to do this exercise using pen and paper, it will be much easier to use a spreadsheet. Only the most basic understanding of the use of spreadsheets is required.

The brief case study used in this activity will also be used in the next three activities.

Case study

Read the case study below.

A friend of yours, Carmela Puccio, is thinking of setting up in business on her own as an architect and has come to you for advice.

Carmela is a qualified architect who currently works for a large firm. She has been approached by one of the firm's clients who is particularly impressed with her work. This client has offered her a 12 month job worth £300 a month should she decide to set up on her own. In addition to this, she estimates she will bill a further £200 in June and £400 in July and August.

Carmela will need to give three months notice and so would start trading on 1 June 2003. You sit down with Carmela and make a note of the following forecasts about her first three months of trading:

- She will work from home for the first three months.
- She will need to advertise to build up trade; this will cost her £500 in June and £200 quarterly after that.

- ◆ Direct costs of materials, travelling etc. will amount to 10 per cent of the sales value for each job.
- ◆ Stocks of materials will cost her £300.
- ◆ Carmela will invoice her customers as soon as work is completed and allow them 30 days credit. As many of her customers may take a few days extra credit, she assumes that customer payment will be received in the second month after the work is done.
- ◆ She anticipates she will be allowed 30 days credit by the suppliers of her direct costs and so will pay in the month following the supply of goods or services.
- ◆ Accountancy costs of £600 will be payable three months after the end of the first year of trading.
- ◆ Other costs will amount to £200 a month.
- ◆ She will purchase a computer and other equipment with a life of four years for £4,000 in June.
- ◆ She will put £6,000 into the business bank account to start the business.

Task

Based on your discussion with Carmela, your task is to prepare a cash flow forecast for her first three months of trading.

Hot tip

Work through all the information gathered from your discussion with Carmela and for each item ask yourself the question, 'Will it appear on her bank statement in the first three months?' Only if the answer is yes should you include it on your cash flow forecast.

Feedback

You may have found this first numerical exercise quite difficult. Trace through all the numbers in the suggested solution shown in Table 1.3 so that you can see where they come from.

Carmela is allowing her customers 60 days credit so the only cash she will actually receive in the first three months is the £500 from her June sales – £300 from her long-term contract and £200 from other work.

To do her job she will need a stock of stationery and other materials. She will be using and replacing these materials all the time but the £300 is needed for her to get started.

Suppliers are paid for other materials a month in arrears so payments start in July. We are assuming that she does not receive any credit for advertising and other costs. Carmela is working from home and so there is no rent.

The capital expenditure on the computer and other equipment is needed as soon as the business starts.

The net cash flow is simply the total of cash received less payments made. Outflows need to be deducted from the opening bank balance to arrive at the forecast closing bank balance. Only in July does she receive more than she pays and so her closing bank balance increases during the month.

	June £	July £	August £	Total £
Cash receipts	–	–	500	500
Payments				
Stock	300	–	–	300
Other materials	–	50	70	120
Advertising	500	–	–	500
Rent	–	–	–	–
Other costs	200	200	200	600
	1,000	250	270	1,520
Capital expenditure	4,000	–	–	4,000
	5,000	250	270	5,520
Net cash flow	(5,000)	(250)	230	(5,020)
Opening bank balance	6,000	1,000	750	6,000
Closing bank balance	1,000	750	980	980

Table 1.3 *Carmela Puccio: forecast cash flow statement for the three months ended 31 August 2003*

But is it profitable?

Profit is the most widely reported measure of business performance, used both by external investors and within companies.

It is what is left over after all expenses have been paid. A product is profitable if it sells for more than it costs to make. Similarly, a service provided by a company is profitable if it can be sold for more than it costs to provide.

So far so good. The only real difficulties come in deciding what to include as an expense and, in particular, when to include it. There are conventions governing how the figure for profit should be arrived at and it is these that are the subject of this section. If finance is the common language of business, then it is essential that managers understand what the financial figures are telling them.

> The managers of a business unit have put in a proposal for the launch of a new product line.
>
> This product will sell 240 units a year for two years. Machinery costing £5,000 will need to be purchased. Because of its specialised nature, this machinery will have no value at the end of the two years.
>
> Units will sell for £20 each and the cost of producing one unit will be £8. No credit will be given to customers nor provided by suppliers.
>
> *Should senior management give the go-ahead for the launch of the new product?*

Remembering from the last section that cash is king, business unit managers produce a cash flow forecast for the first twelve months. This is shown in Table 1.4.

		Year 1 £
Cash in from customers	240 x £20	4,800
Cash out: machinery		5,000
other costs	240 x £8	1,920
		6,920
Net cash flow		(2,120)

Table 1.4 *Cash flow forecast for Year 1*

This cash flow statement shows income of £4,800 but outgoings of £6,920 and so a net outflow of cash of £2,120. On these figures it might appear that the new product line launch should be abandoned.

But there is something wrong in this argument. Look at the cash flow statement for both years, shown in Table 1.5.

	Year 1 £	Year 2 £	Combined £
Cash in from customers	4,800	4,800	9,600
Cash out: machinery	5,000	–	5,000
other costs	1,920	1,920	3,840
	6,920	1,920	8,840
Net cash flow	(2,120)	2,880	760

Table 1.5 *Cash flow forecast for Years 1 and 2*

Year 2 shows a positive cash flow; why is this?

The reason is that the machine was paid for in Year 1 but used for the whole of the two years. In Year 2, the cash flow is positive because the business is using the machine but does not have to pay for it again.

Comparing profit and cash flow statements

Profit statements attempt to match sales with the costs incurred in making those sales, irrespective of when the actual cash receipts and payments took place.

Continuing our example, the machine has a life span of two years and so its cost should be spread over two years, as shown in Table 1.6.

	Year 1 £	Year 2 £	Combined £
Sales	4,800	4,800	9,600
Expenses: depreciation	2,500	2,500	5,000
other costs	1,920	1,920	3,840
	4,420	4,420	8,840
Profit	380	380	760

Table 1.6 *Profit and loss account for Years 1 and 2*

Compare the two statements shown in Tables 1.5 and 1.6. What is different and what is the same?

The differences between the cash flow statement and the profit and loss account (to give our two projections their full names) are as follows:

◆ 'Sales' are what has been invoiced to customers. In our simple example we have presumed they paid cash and so this figure agrees with the amount of cash received. If the business sells on credit, then the figure for sales in the profit and loss account will not equal the figure for cash received from customers on the cash flow statement.

◆ 'Depreciation' is the charge made for the use of plant and other equipment during the year. In this case the machinery cost £5,000, had a life of two years and so we charged £2,500 a year.

◆ For the two years combined, the net cash flow and profit figures are the same and this is true of all businesses in the long run.

The differences between the cash flow statement and the profit and loss account are *timing* differences, the revenues (or sales) and the expenses can appear in the two statements in different periods.

Finally, note that our profit and loss account is based on the assumption that the machinery will only have a life of two years. This is a matter of judgement, others may consider the equipment has a life of three, four or even five years. In this case the depreciation figure would be much less as we would be spreading the cost over more years. Many figures in the profit and loss account are based upon this sort of subjective judgement and so it is always important to know the assumptions used in preparing the figures.

Using different performance measures

If cash is king, why go to all the trouble of producing a profit and loss account?

There are accountants and commentators who argue that the profit figures reported by companies are meaningless and that companies should just report the 'hard' numbers shown on the cash flow statement. We will return to this topic in a later section but will, for the moment, consider the relative merits of our two statements.

We clearly need the cash flow statement both because if we run out of cash we will go bankrupt and because we want to know how much cash we will have available for future projects.

However, we also want to know whether what we are producing is profitable – if something costs more to make than we can sell it for, then in the long run we have no future, however cleverly we manage our cash position. We also want to know whether our businesses are becoming more profitable or less profitable, and to find out we need at some stage to compare the profit for the current year with that for the previous year.

So, what we need to do is look at both statements, and this is true of financial statements and financial measures in general. They are all different ways of looking at the same picture and, as long as we understand them, can all provide useful information for making better decisions.

Activity 3
Forecast profit and loss account

Objectives

This activity asks you to prepare the forecast profit and loss account for Carmela.

At the end of this activity, you will be able to:

◆ prepare a forecast profit and loss account statement

◆ evaluate cash flow forecasts.

Task

Using the case study material about Carmela Puccio in Activity 2, prepare Carmela's forecast profit and loss account for the first three months of her new business.

Hot tip

First establish the sales for the three months. This is the total amount that will be invoiced to customers for work carried out during this period.

Then review the information provided by Carmela, asking yourself, 'What expenses were incurred during the period?' – what expenditure was necessary in order to make the sales or run the business. Completely ignore whether or not any money was actually paid during the three months.

Feedback

	£	£
Sales		1,900
Cost of sales		190
Gross profit		1,710
Expenses		
Advertising	500	
Rent	–	
Accountancy	150	
Depreciation	250	
Other costs	600	1,500
Net profit/(loss)		£210

Table 1.7 *Carmela Puccio: forecast trading and profit and loss account for the three months ended 31 August 2003*

Carmela's forecast profit and loss account for the first three months is shown in Table 1.7.

Sales are the amounts invoiced for the first three months, 3 x £300 for the long-term client and £1,000 for other billing.

Cost of sales is forecast to be 10 per cent of sales. The stock will still be in hand at the end of the period and so this is not charged as an expense. The advertising and other costs have been both charged as an expense and paid for during the period. The accountancy costs will not be paid until August in 2004, but they are still a necessary expense of the business and a charge of £150 must be made for the first quarter, that is, the annual charge of £600 divided by four. This is an accrual, or we say we have 'accrued' the accountancy charge. Accruals are where an expense has been incurred but there is no specific invoice relating to the charge for the period.

The depreciation is for the use of the computer and other equipment during this three-month period. The total cost was £4,000, the computer has a life of four years and so £1,000 must be charged each year. Our forecast profit and loss account is for three months and so we must make a charge of £250.

This leaves Carmela with a profit of £210.

Making assets work harder

Whether a particular level of profit represents a 'good' result for a business depends partly on the investment required to make that profit. A profit of half a million pounds each year for a local business may be excellent. The same profit for a quoted company with tens of millions of pounds of assets would be a very poor result indeed.

Making a return on assets

If your aunt left you £10,000 in her will and you had a choice of two deposit accounts in which to place the money, you would choose the one that gave the highest return. So if one account paid, say, £400 per annum and the other £500 per annum, you would clearly go for the one that paid £500.

Similarly in business – those who invest in the stock market or directly in companies are looking for the highest return they can get. The directors of companies are therefore under pressure to produce the highest profit they can from the assets employed in the business.

Consider two business opportunities, Project X and Project Y, both generating cash flows of £1,000 a year. Project X requires an investment in state-of-the-art machinery which will cost £50,000. Project Y can use machinery which is widely available and which will cost only £10,000. Clearly, all other things being equal, Project Y is a more attractive investment than Project X: a lesser investment is required for the same return.

In summary, at any time, management are trying to:

- increase revenue without increasing the assets employed in the business, and/or
- decrease the assets employed in the business whilst maintaining the same revenue.

Types of assets

The assets employed in a business are summarised in an organisation's balance sheet. Before looking at a balance sheet, we will describe the typical assets employed in a business.

Fixed assets

Fixed assets include any assets bought for long-term use within the business. They will include:

- any offices or buildings owned or leased by the business
- plant and machinery, including IT equipment
- fixtures and fittings used in offices
- any motor vehicles.

Assets which are classified as 'fixed assets' for one business may be classified as 'stock items' for another. For example, a shop selling personal computers will treat these as stock items as they have been bought by the shop with a view to selling them on to end customers. The businesses that buy the computers will treat them as fixed assets, as they will be used within the businesses in sales, administration or production to help run the business.

Current assets

In Figure 1.1, the 'Actions' box shows the actual activity taking place within a manufacturing company. Raw materials are being delivered to the site, being converted into finished goods and shipped to customers. The customers are then invoiced and after 30 or more days payment is received.

15

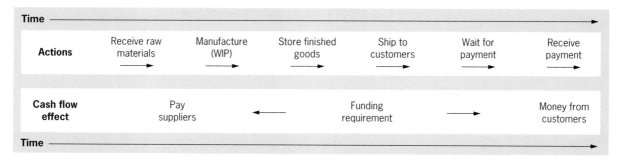

Figure 1.1 *The trading cycle*

The second box, 'Cash flow effect', shows the impact of all this activity on the company's bank balance. The effect starts after the delivery of the goods as the company is given credit by its suppliers. From the moment the company pays its suppliers, however, there is a funding requirement until payment is received from customers.

In order for a company to trade, it will have money tied up in assets employed in the trading cycle. These assets are only held for the short term and are therefore known as **current assets** or **working capital**.

To illustrate what we mean by the trading cycle, consider a company manufacturing components for a car manufacturer. It must buy in raw materials if it is to manufacture. On the factory floor at any one time there will be partially finished components known as work-in-progress (WIP). In the goods outwards area there will be finished components waiting to be shipped.

The raw materials, WIP and finished goods comprise the stock held by the company. Even when the stock is shipped to customers the company's requirement for current assets does not end. This is because it will sell on credit to the car manufacturers and so it will have funds tied up in debtors. Debtors (also known as accounts receivable) are the amounts the company is owed by its customers at a point in time.

It is not all bad news, however. In the same way that the company offers credit to its customers, it will be offered credit by its suppliers. Creditors (also known as accounts payable) are the amounts a company owes its suppliers at a point in time. Creditors are liabilities – an amount owed by the company to a third party.

Finally, the company will need to hold a certain amount of money available at the bank to pay suppliers and expenses as they fall due. This money will be topped up by the money received from its customers as they settle invoices.

Assets held by different businesses

We have used a traditional manufacturing business to describe the different types of current assets a business will hold. Current assets will be grouped under these headings in all businesses, but the nature and the relative size of the assets will vary greatly. Service industries will almost always have funds tied up in stock or debtors, as the case of Dennis illustrates.

Dennis is thinking of using his skills to set up in business maintaining older photocopiers for local businesses.

He thinks that by the end of the first year he will have 160 customers each paying him £20 a month under a contract for his services.

He will need to keep a stock of parts on hand which will cost him £2,000 to purchase when he starts the business. Once he has made the initial purchase, then he will use and replace about £250 worth of parts each month so that the stock of parts held at any time will continue to be worth £2,000.

He intends to keep at least £500 in the bank to meet any immediate cash needs.

Finally, in order to carry on his business he will need a van and some tools. He thinks he can buy a van for about £4,000 and that the necessary tools will cost him about £300.

Draw up a list of the assets Dennis will employ in his business at the end of the first year.

Let us assume that Dennis is going to give his customers 30 days credit and obtain the same length of credit from his suppliers. This then gives us the statement shown in Table 1.8.

	£	£
Fixed assets		
Van	4,000	
Tools	300	4,300
Current assets		
Stock (of spare parts)	2,000	
Debtors (160 x £20)	3,200	
Cash	500	
	5,700	
Less: Creditors (for the spare parts)	250	5,450
Total net assets		**£9,750**

Table 1.8 *Dennis: statement of assets at end of year*

Make sure you understand how each of the figures on this statement is calculated. If you have any problems, ask a colleague or someone from your finance department.

What we have done here is to produce a snapshot of the business at a future point in time. What we are saying is that on the basis of the assumptions Dennis is making, these will be the assets employed in the business on a specific date.

Returning to our discussion at the beginning of this section, we can also say that Dennis will require an investment of £9,750 to operate this business. This is because all assets must be funded in some way.

In what ways could Dennis reduce the amount of investment needed to run his business?

Dennis will have limited funds and needs to think carefully about how to reduce the investment in his new business. Possible actions might include:

◆ buying an older van to use until the business becomes established

◆ agreeing that customers pay annually in advance for a maintenance contract rather than monthly in arrears

◆ reducing the amount of money invested in spare parts – could he make some new agreement with suppliers for shorter delivery times?

Reading financial statements

The order in which the assets were summarised in the example from Dennis follows the usual UK conventions for preparing a company's balance sheet. Remember that finance forms a common language for business and so following accepted conventions for presentation makes financial statements more readily understandable.

The amounts against each asset type are simply what Dennis has told us, they are not the result of any specialist accountant's calculations. If Dennis is saying he will be billing 160 customers £20 a month and they pay a month in arrears, then they will owe a total of £3,200 at the end of any month.

This contains an important message for all non-accountant managers. All items in the financial statements, particularly at business unit level, should be easy for everyone to understand. Managers should expect and demand explanations that enable them to understand every item from those preparing the financial statements.

Let us change some of Dennis' assumptions and consider the effects of the changes on his assets:

1 If the van only costs him £2,500, what are the total net assets employed in the business?

2 If his customers pay after 60 days rather than 30 days, what will be the balance sheet figure for debtors?

3 If he uses and replaces spare parts that cost £500 a month, how much will he owe his suppliers at any one time?

The effects of the above changes on Dennis' assets are as follows:

1 The van is costing him £1,500 less than he originally thought and so his total net assets will be £1,500 less, which comes to £8,250 (£9,750 – £1,500).

2 At any one time, debtors will now equal two months' sales, which equals £6,400.

3 Creditors will equal £500 as he pays for this month's spare parts next month. Dennis also needs to consider whether his stock figure of £2,000 is high enough because the more spare parts he uses, the greater the number of spare parts he is likely to need to have on hand at any point in time.

Activity 4
The forecast balance sheet

Objectives

By the end of this activity you will have prepared a forecast statement of the assets in a business and have had an introduction to the balance sheet.

When you have completed this activity, you will be able to:

◆ prepare a simple forecast balance sheet

◆ explain what is included under the different balance sheet headings.

Task

Using the case study material about Carmela Puccio in Activity 2, prepare a list of Carmela's forecast assets:

◆ at the commencement of the business on her first day of trading

◆ at the close of business on 31 August 2003.

Hot tip

Remember that you are preparing a list of the assets of the business at a point in time. Think about what assets are employed in the business at the two dates and how you might verify that they exist.

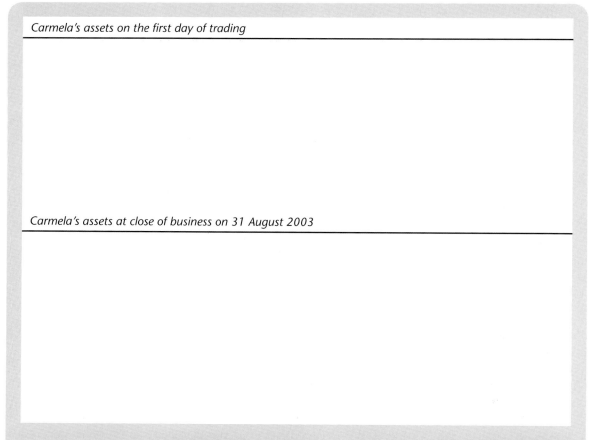

Carmela's assets on the first day of trading

Carmela's assets at close of business on 31 August 2003

Feedback

At the commencement of business on the first day of trading, the balance sheet will be as shown in Table 1.9.

Current assets	
Bank balance	£6,000
Funded by:	
Opening capital	£6,000

Table 1.9 *Carmela Puccio: forecast balance sheet at 9.00 a.m. on 1 June 2003*

Carmela has yet to start trading or buy any fixed assets or stock. The only asset of the business is the £6,000 she has deposited in a new business account. All assets must be funded in some way. In Carmela's case, this represents money put into the business by the owner, which we call capital.

The forecast balance sheet for Carmela will be as shown in Table 1.10.

	£	£	£
Fixed assets			
At cost			4,000
Less: depreciation			250
			3,750
Current assets			
Stock		300	
Debtors		1,400	
Bank balance		980	
		2,680	
Current liabilities			
Creditors	70		
Accrual	150	(220)	
			2,460
			£6,210
Funded by:			
Opening capital			6,000
Add: profit for year			210
			£6,210

Table 1.10 *Carmela Puccio: forecast balance sheet at 31 August 2003*

Feedback

As some new terms have been introduced with this statement, we will take each heading in turn:

Fixed assets: at cost	what the assets originally cost the business – in an established business this may be years back in time
Fixed assets: depreciation	less the depreciation charged over time to the profit and loss account. See previous section 'But is it profitable' on calculating the profit for an explanation of depreciation
Stock	the amount forecast by Carmela
Debtors	invoice from July, £700, and August, £700, remain unpaid – total £1,400

Bank balance	as per the cash flow forecast we prepared in Activity 2
Creditors	Carmela owes her suppliers for August's direct material costs of £70
Accrual	an accrual is exactly the same as a creditor except the business has not received an invoice. In our example, this is the charge for accountancy in the profit and loss account which Carmela does not expect to pay until next year

The funding side of the balance sheet is further explained in the next section. For the moment note that:

Opening capital	is the money deposited in the bank to start the business
Profit	selling goods or services at a profit provides the major source of new funding for businesses. The figure agrees with that set out in Carmela's forecast profit and loss account

Again, trace through where the different numbers come from on the forecast balance sheet. At this stage, you may wish to go back to Activity 2 and try again to produce all three of the forecast statements for Carmela – it will be an excellent way of consolidating your understanding!

Looking at the total picture

In this section we will prepare the forecast cash flow, profit and loss account and asset summary for a new business venture. This is useful to establish a clearer picture of the links between the three different financial statements and present a more complete financial picture of a business.

Preparing a financial plan

The numbers used in the example will be simple, but the process we will carry out is close to that actually used by any business that is considering launching a new venture. You may associate financial information with pages of figures, but when considering any new venture it is best to start with some key assumptions and elaborate on the numbers at a later time.

You may also think of accounting as primarily concerned with looking at the financial accounts of the previous year and wonder why we are spending so much time on looking at financial projections rather than historical numbers.

Historical and forecast financial information is usually prepared and presented in the same way and so everything learnt in this theme applies equally to both types of information.

The underlying assumptions

The first step in preparing any plan, whether financial or not, is to carefully consider the key assumptions on which the plan will be based. From these basic assumptions it is then possible to start building the first draft financial projections.

These financial projections have been made very much easier to prepare with the introduction of computer spreadsheets. These spreadsheets are the modern equivalent of 'back of the envelope' calculations which enable people to see quickly whether a possible venture is worth investigating further.

Pearce Joinery is a well-established business considering branching out into the construction of exhibition stands for conference organisers. The new business will commence next April. As its financial adviser, you have been asked to attend a preliminary meeting to discuss some ideas and prepare financial projections for the first six months of trading. Sitting down with its managers, you note down some of their key thoughts and assumptions about the new venture.

The company will employ a full-time salesperson to build up the new business, at a cost to the company of £24,000 per annum. The salesperson will be supported by a part-time administrator at a cost of £12,000 per annum.

The marketing department forecasts that the company should have two customers per month for the first three months and three customers per month for the second three months. These customers will be charged an average of £5,000 per month each, with payment due within 30 days.

Material costs for each job will average out at £1,000 per job and other costs at £500 per job. The direct labour which will work on the contracts will be drawn from the main business and will cost about 50 per cent of the amount billed.

It will be necessary to purchase stocks of materials costing £4,000 and a vehicle costing £8,000. To start the business, the existing management intends to open up a new bank account into which it will deposit £20,000.

This is sufficient information to draw up forecast cash flow, profit and loss account and balance sheet statements. To make the steps in preparing the forecasts clear, let us first draw up a summary of the main income, Table 1.11, and outgoings, Table 1.12, month by month.

	Sales £	Cash received £
April	10,000	0
May	10,000	10,000
June	10,000	10,000
July	15,000	10,000
August	15,000	15,000
September	15,000	15,000
	75,000	**60,000**

Table 1.11 *Pearce Joinery: sales forecast*

A sales forecast is our best estimate of the total value of the amount billed to customers. We will look at sales forecasts in more depth in the next theme: Preparing and monitoring budgets.

The sales forecast shown in Table 1.11 is based on the company invoicing two customers for the first three months and three customers in each of the subsequent three months. 'Sales' represents the amount invoiced to customers, irrespective of whether or not the money has been received. For the cash flow statement we will need to know exactly what money has been paid into the bank. Here, because customers take 30 days credit, the company will not receive any money in April and will be owed £15,000 at the end of September for the sales made in that month.

	Labour costs £	Material costs £	Other costs £	Payments for materials £
April	5,000	2,000	1,000	0
May	5,000	2,000	1,000	2,000
June	5,000	2,000	1,000	2,000
July	7,500	3,000	1,500	2,000
August	7,500	3,000	1,500	3,000
September	7,500	3,000	1,500	3,000
	37,500	**15,000**	**7,500**	**12,000**

Table 1.12 *Pearce Joinery: expenses*

The expenses month by month, shown in Table 1.12, are again taken from the discussion with management. Note that for this sort of forecasting it is quite usual to express costs such as labour as a percentage of income; it is a broad-brush approach but then these are broad-brush figures.

We are assuming here that labour and other costs are paid in the month in which the expenditure is incurred. The suppliers of materials allow 30 days credit. The company will therefore make no payment in April but owe £3,000 at the end of September for the materials used in that month.

The cash flow forecast

We are now in a position to draw up the cash flow forecast. Remember that cash flow forecasts are simply about what we anticipate will go through the business's bank account. The cash flow forecast for Pearce Joinery is shown in Table 1.13.

	£	
Cash in		
From customers	60,000	see sales forecasts
Cash out		
Salesperson	12,000	6 months per discussion
Administrator	6,000	6 months per discussion
Labour	37,500	see expenses
Materials	12,000	see expenses
Other costs	7,500	see expenses
Stock	4,000	see discussion
Vehicle	8,000	see discussion
	87,000	
Net cash inflow/outflow	**(27,000)**	
Opening balance at bank	20,000	see discussion
Closing balance at bank	**(7,000)**	

Table 1.13 *Pearce Joinery: cash flow forecast for the six months to 30 September*

Showing the £27,000 net cash flow in brackets denotes that it is money going out of the business. The brackets around the £7,000 closing bank balance denote that Pearce Joinery is overdrawn. You will find in financial statements and reports that brackets are used to highlight different things in different circumstances and it is often necessary, perhaps with the use of a calculator, to work out for yourself what they show.

Make sure you understand where each number on the cash flow statement comes from; all the bold figures without a note against them are totals or subtotals. If you have difficulty, ask a member of your finance department to help you.

What the cash flow forecast tells us is that during the first six months, cheques paid out of the bank account will exceed money banked by £27,000. As the business was started with only £20,000 in the bank, then by the end of September we can expect the business to be £7,000 overdrawn.

It should come as no surprise that the cash flow is negative for the first period of trading. When a new business starts, it will take time for sales to build up. Research shows that one of the main reasons new businesses fail is that the managers are too optimistic about the speed with which they will build a customer base, causing them to run out of money before they reach critical mass.

The other main reason that cash flows are negative is that businesses have to invest in assets in order to start the business. In the case of Pearce Joinery, it must find the money both for the vehicle and for a stock of materials before it can start work.

The forecast profit and loss account

So we know that cash flows are negative for the first six months, but is this a profitable business? The profit and loss account for Pearce Joinery is shown in Table 1.14.

	£	
Sales	75,000	see sales forecasts
Expenses		
Salesperson	12,000	6 months per discussion
Administrator	6,000	6 months per discussion
Labour	37,500	see expenses
Materials	15,000	see expenses
Other costs	7,500	see expenses
Depreciation	1,000	see next paragraph
	79,000	
Profit/(loss)	(4,000)	

Table 1.14 *Pearce Joinery: profit and loss account for the six months to 30 September*

Again, make sure that you know the origin of all the numbers in these statements. We know that the van cost £8,000 and will last for four years, so to be fair we must charge £2,000 as an expense in each of these four years. This profit and loss account is only for six months and so we will charge half the annual charge, £1,000.

It appears the new venture is not profitable. However, sales are building up and there are certain fixed costs which must be met however little or much the company sells. These fixed costs are the salaries of the salesperson and the administrator plus the depreciation on the vehicle. It may be possible to increase sales to five or six contracts a month and not increase these fixed costs. We will return to the important relationship between profit and the level of activity later.

The forecast balance sheet

Our final statement is the balance sheet. The assets side of the balance sheet comprises the fixed assets and the current assets.

The principle behind the balance sheet is that all assets employed in a business must have been funded in some way and so the total of this funding will always equal the assets employed in a business.

The focus of this book is more on your responsibilities for the management of the assets employed in the business than the funding side of the equation; if you are part of a large group, it is quite likely that your unit is simply funded by head office. However, for completeness we will look at the forecast balance sheet for Pearce Joinery, Table 1.15.

	£	£	£
Fixed assets			
Vehicle at cost		8,000	
Less: depreciation		1,000	
			7,000
Current assets			
Stock	4,000		
Debtors	15,000		
		19,000	
Less: Creditors	3,000		
Bank overdraft	7,000		
		(10,000)	
			9,000
			16,000
Funded by			
Opening capital			20,000
Profit/(loss) for six months			(4,000)
			16,000

Table 1.15 *Pearce Joinery: balance sheet as at 30 September*

Again, make sure you understand the origin of the numbers. What is most important is that you are aware that the figures in the balance sheet shown in Table 1.15 are not some figment of the accountant's imagination but represent real assets and liabilities which it is the responsibility of the manager to control.

We will briefly look at each item in the balance sheet in turn.

Vehicle at cost
What the vehicle originally cost the company

Less depreciation
Vehicles wear out, so we subtract here the depreciation we charged as an expense in the profit and loss account

Stock
At any one time, the company holds a stock of materials ready to start or complete a job

Debtors
The amount of money customers owe at 30 September – see the sales forecast, Table 1.11

Creditors
The amount the company owes to suppliers at the balance sheet date – see the expenses, Table 1.12

Bank overdraft
The amount the company owes the bank

Opening capital
The money introduced to start the business – in this case it was the £20,000 deposited in the bank

Profit or loss for period
Profit is a source of funds for the business

Whilst profit is a source of funds for the business, making a loss uses up the capital or reserves of the business – as is the case for Pearce Joinery in the first six months of trading.

This concludes the introduction to the three main financial statements.

Activity 5
Reviewing the financial forecasts

Objectives

In this activity we will stand back and review the three financial statements we have prepared for Carmela.

When you have completed this activity, you will be able to:

◆ analyse financial statements

◆ advise on appropriate courses of action.

Task

Review the three financial forecasts you prepared for Carmela Puccio in Activities 2–4; these are reproduced here. Make a list of matters you wish to discuss with her at your follow-up meeting.

	June £	July £	August £	Total £
Cash receipts	–	–	500	500
Payments				
Stock	300	–	–	300
Other materials	–	50	70	120
Advertising	500	–	–	500
Rent	–	–	–	–
Other costs	200	200	200	600
	1,000	250	270	1,520
Capital expenditure	4,000	–	–	4,000
	5,000	250	270	5,520
Net cash flow	(5,000)	(250)	230	(5,020)
Opening bank balance	6,000	1,000	750	6,000
Closing bank balance	1,000	750	980	980

Table 1.16 *Carmela Puccio: forecast cash flow statement for the three months ended 31 August 2003*

	£	£
Sales		1,900
Cost of sales		190
Gross profit		1,710
Expenses		
Advertising	500	
Rent	–	
Accountancy	150	
Depreciation	250	
Other costs	600	
		(1,500)
Net profit/(loss)		210

Table 1.17 *Carmela Puccio: forecast trading and profit and loss account for the three months ended 31 August 2003*

	£	£	£
Fixed assets			
At cost			4,000
Less: depreciation			250
			3,750
Current assets			
Stock		300	
Debtors		1,400	
Bank balance		980	
		2,680	
Current liabilities			
Creditors	70		
Accrual	150	(220)	
			2,460
			6,210
Funded by:			
Opening capital			6,000
Add: profit for year			210
			6,210

Table 1.18 *Carmela Puccio: forecast balance sheet at 31 August 2003*

Matters to discuss with Carmela in the light of your review:

Feedback

A number of issues could be raised. Here are some of them:

1 The business is profitable but is it profitable enough for Carmela's private expenses? Her ultimate objective must be to take sufficient money out of the business to live on. Clearly £210 profit during the first three months of trading is not sufficient to do this. She may be taking a realistic view about the length of time it will take to build up her client base, so longer-term projections are needed before she takes any decision to go ahead.

2 As we have already seen, a cash outflow is almost inevitable during the first months of trading for any new business. The £6,000 she introduces into the business will cover her forecast net cash outflows during the first three months of trading. However, has she additional funds available to cover her living expenses during this period?

3 Is Carmela spending enough on marketing? Given the need to generate sales and income, should she be more ambitious in her plans to find customers? Even if this meant taking out a bank loan, the quicker build-up in business may be worth it.

4 Have all her costs really been included? In particular, she has not included any costs for travelling or entertaining. Both of these may be important items as she works at attracting new clients.

◆ Recap

Explore why cash planning is essential to running a business and practise preparing a cash flow forecast

◆ A cash flow forecast is a projection of the cash flowing into and out of a business over a specific period of time.

◆ The cash flow forecast enables you to identify points where the business may either need additional cash infusions or have cash surpluses for further investment.

Discover how profit measurement differs from cash flow and why both profit and cash are essential indicators of business performance

◆ Profit is the difference between revenue earned and costs incurred.

◆ The difference between profit and cash is timing. When measuring profit, sales are matched with the costs, irrespective of when the costs were actually incurred or the cash for the goods or services sold was received.

Practise preparing a profit and loss account forecast

◆ The profit and loss account shows how much profit or loss is made by the business over a period of time.

◆ It shows:
  – sales – cost of sales = gross profit
  – gross profit – expenses = net profit.

Learn about the main types of assets in a business

◆ Fixed assets are assets which are bought for long-term use by the business.

◆ Current assets are items such as cash, stock and debtors that are currently cash or expected to be turned into cash within one year.

Prepare a simple forecast balance sheet

◆ The balance sheet is an indicator of the financial position of a business at a given moment in time.

◆ It lists the organisation's:

    – assets (things owned by the business)

    – liabilities (amounts owed by the business)

    – capital (owner's investment in the business).

◆ The balance sheet is set out in a standard format, which must show that:

assets = liabilities + capital

▶▶ More @

Broadbent, M. and Cullen, J. (2003) *Managing Financial Resources,* Butterworth-Heinemann

Owen, A. (2003) *Accounting for Business Studies,* Butterworth-Heinemann

The above are both wide-ranging texts designed for managers who want to develop their financial management capabilities further – they consider the topics discussed within this book at a more detailed level.

Harvey, D., McLaney, E. and Atrill, P. (2001), *Accounting for Business,* Butterworth-Heinemann

This book focuses more on financial accounting than financial management. Aimed primarily at accounting students, it provides detailed coverage of current accounting practices and legislation.

Bized is an award-winning site providing free learning resources on business and economics related subjects. For a direct link to the accounting and finance section which provides further information on cash, profit and each of the financial statements, with numerous examples, try **www.bized.ac.uk/stafsup/options/acc/acc_g.htm**

The websites for the major banks all have areas dedicated to supporting businesses in managing their finances that provide practical information and advice.

2 Preparing and monitoring budgets

To run any organisation, it is necessary to plan. We must say where we want to go and how we think we can best get there. There will be a financial dimension to nearly all the plans prepared by an organisation and most organisations will prepare annual budgets as part of their business planning activities.

Some organisations, however, are moving away from the traditional, detailed budgeting activity, arguing that the timescales involved in preparing budgets mean that they are often out of date before they are approved. To justify all the effort and resource that goes into financial planning, budgets really must add value by communicating, informing and guiding essential business decisions.

In this theme you explore financial planning. You start by investigating the budget that provides the starting point for all the other financial projections: the sales forecast. You go on to look at expense budgets and finally at how financial planning fits within the context of overall business planning.

In this theme you will:

◆ **Assess the process for drawing up a sales forecast and critically appraise a sales forecast from your organisation**

◆ **Explore the process for setting and managing expense budgets in your organisation**

◆ **Evaluate the benefits and limitations of the financial planning process in your organisation.**

Preparing a sales forecast

All organisations require some form of income to pay for their expenditure. Sales or income forecasting – estimating the level of income you will receive in a given period – is a key input to a business's financial planning process.

Our prime purpose in this section is to look at the process by which the sales forecast is put together and evaluated. We will do this by taking an example and then thinking about what broader conclusions can be drawn.

Homer Products imports a range of three fitness machines from an American manufacturer and sells directly to commercial health clubs and gyms. It has an exclusive dealership for the UK and the sales team is divided between the north and south of the country.

The three products vary according to the number of different exercises that can be done on the same machine and the different ways in which it can be programmed. The basic machine is called the Single, the next one up the range is called the Multi and the premium product is called the Tracker.

This is a brief, very brief, description of the business. When senior managers review the sales forecast they will be looking above all at the credibility of the people who prepared the plan. Are they close to their customers, do they know their product, do they know how the market/technology is moving? However impressive a set of sales forecasts may look on paper, they will be ignored if the directors, venture capitalists or other potential investors do not have faith in the people who prepared the plan.

Last year

An excellent way to increase our understanding of the business is to look at the figures for the previous year. Homer Products' unit sales for last year, Year 1, are shown in Table 2.1.

Table 2.1 shows the number of machines sold, not their value. We can see that unit sales are much higher in the south, particularly at the premium end of the market. It would be interesting to know here the size of the total market and what percentage of that market Homer Products has.

	North	South	Total
Tracker	40	80	120
Multi	60	90	150
Single	100	100	200
	200	**270**	**470**

Table 2.1 *Homer Products: unit sales during Year 1*

Next, we will analyse the sales figure shown in last year's accounts, see Table 2.2.

	Selling price £	North £	South £	Total £
Tracker	5,000	200,000	400,000	600,000
Multi	3,000	180,000	270,000	450,000
Single	2,000	200,000	200,000	400,000
		580,000	870,000	1,450,000

Table 2.2 *Homer Products: sales analysis Year 1*

The figures in Table 2.2 are calculated simply by multiplying the unit sales by the selling price for each of the three products.

The accounts of the company for the last year show a profit of £175,000, see Table 2.3.

	£
Sales	1,450,000
Expenses	
Purchases	725,000
Marketing	300,000
Other costs	250,000
	1,275,000
Profit	175,000

Table 2.3 *Homer Products: profit and loss account Year 1*

The statement shown in Table 2.3 shows that the company operates on a 100 per cent mark-up on everything it imports from America – this can be confirmed in discussion but appears to be true because the sales figure is twice that for purchases. Marketing costs represent the major additional expense and the business appears profitable with net profit equal to approximately 12 per cent of sales.

Next year

Having learnt something about the company and looked at last year's figures, we now need to consider what the outlook is for the coming year, Year 2.

Prospects for the coming year
The overall economic outlook is good, with growth in the national economy forecast at 2.5 per cent and inflation at 2.0 per cent.

Market research shows growth in the opening of new gyms slowing in the south but continuing to be buoyant in the north, with growth rates of 2 per cent and 10 per cent respectively. The types of products purchased in each region are expected to show more equal profiles.

` Any substantial growth in unit sales will need a 20 per cent increase in marketing costs.

Looking to the longer term, the dealership agreement with the American manufacturer has another five years to run. Sales enquiries are coming in from continental Europe and the marketing director is eager to start sales in this area. This would involve renegotiating the dealership agreement and a substantial increase in marketing expenditure.

From this information we must produce the first draft of the sales forecast.

Two things are immediately apparent:

◆ we would like to have more information

◆ there is no 'right' answer.

There is always more potential information that might be useful in preparing a forecast and no two people are ever likely to agree completely on what should be in the sales forecast.

One possible forecast is provided in Table 2.4.

Unit sales			North	South	Total
Tracker			48	88	136
Multi			72	99	171
Single			100	100	200
Total Year 2			**220**	**287**	**507**
Total Year 1			*200*	*270*	*470*

Sales	Selling price per unit £	North £	South £	Total £
Tracker	5,100	244,800	448,800	693,600
Multi	3,060	220,320	302,940	523,260
Single	2,040	204,000	204,000	408,000
Total Year 2		**669,120**	**955,740**	**1,624,860**
Total Year 1		*580,000*	*870,000*	*1,450,000*

Assumptions
2% price increase across the board
Tracker and Multi – 20% increase north, 10% south
Single – no volume increase

Table 2.4 *Homer Products: sales forecast Year 2*

No two people or marketing teams are ever likely to come up with exactly the same sales forecast. What is important is that all members of the team understand how the figures have been built up and are willing to own them. By 'own' we mean a belief in the figures and the ability to stand up to a critical examination of how the forecast has been put together.

Activity 6
Your organisation's sales forecast

Objectives

In this activity you will learn how to:

◆ contribute to the preparation of a sales or income forecast

◆ critically appraise a sales or income forecast produced by others.

Task

Investigate how the sales or income forecast or budget for your
business unit, company or organisation is put together. Concentrate as
far as possible on the forecast for the sales which most directly provide
the income which pays for your own department.

Find out the following:

Who is responsible for preparing the sales forecast and who provides input for its preparation?

Who is responsible for approving the sales forecast?

How the sales forecast is analysed; is it by:

◆ geographical region?

◆ product?

◆ sales team?

◆ some other way?

What does the way sales are analysed say about your business?

Feedback

The procedures for producing sales forecasts will vary from organisation to organisation. This is because different types of businesses require different approaches and also for internal historical or political reasons.

1 Normally, the marketing department will be responsible for the sales forecast or budget. Many other departments may have some input. For instance, the manufacturing or operations departments will need to say whether it is practical to produce what the sales department say they can sell. Again, there may be a research or economics department within your organisation providing input on the economic outlook for the markets in which your organisation operates.

2 The sales forecast may be presented by the marketing manager to the senior management team of your organisation. Ultimately, your sales forecast may need to be approved by divisional or head office directors.

3 Sales may be analysed in more than one way – they may be analysed once by geographical region and once by product. Depending on the nature of the business, sales may be analysed in any number of ways. For instance, if your organisation only sells to a few major customers, sales forecasts may be built up customer by customer.

4 The way sales are analysed can say a lot about how a business views itself. For example, whereas the emphasis in the past may have been on local autonomy, with forecasts built up country by country, there may now be increasing focus on global product management. Thus a change in the way sales forecasts are presented may reflect fundamental changes in the focus of a business.

Controlling an expense budget

The sales forecast forms the basis of the sales budget. Expense budgets refer to all the expenditure in an organisation other than that directly associated with sales.

For instance, in a manufacturing organisation there will be different expense budgets for marketing, finance, production planning, human resources and research, but purchases of raw materials will be budgeted separately. In a financial services organisation the expense budgets will cover similar overhead expenditure but not the financing costs of the business.

It is part of the function of managers that they hold responsibility for the department or area under their control. Where this area of control includes financial responsibilities, the financial reporting system needs to be designed in such a way that the manager's performance can be assessed. As part of being held to account, the manager will usually hold an expense budget and receive monthly reports of actual expenditure against the budget originally agreed.

Setting the budget

There is a sequence to the effective running of an expense budget. See Figure 2.1.

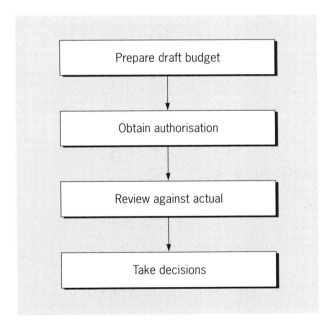

Figure 2.1 *Sequence for running an expense budget*

To illustrate these steps, we will again take a look at a short case study. A company is halfway through its financial year and the manager of the marketing department is reviewing the accountant's latest report on his expense budget, see Table 2.5.

39

Report for the six months ending 30 June					
		6 months		12 months	
	Actual	Budget	Variance	Forecast	Budget
	£	£	£	£	£
Marketing personnel salaries	60,000	70,000	10,000	130,000	140,000
Support staff salaries	30,000	27,500	(2,500)	60,000	55,000
Travelling	8,000	6,000	(2,000)	12,000	12,000
Telephone	3,000	2,500	(500)	5,000	5,000
Other office expenses	2,000	2,250	250	4,000	4,500
Training and conferences	5,000	7,000	2,000	12,000	14,000
	108,000	115,250	7,250	223,000	230,500

Table 2.5 *Marketing department expense budget*

The six months' actual figures are taken from the accounting records of the business and represent what has actually been spent. The marketing manager, let us call him John, will review these figures carefully to ensure no items of expenditure have been charged by mistake to his department.

The budget for the six months and the 12 months will be the figures agreed during the budgeting exercise the previous year. The variance is the budgeted spend for the six months less the actual spend.

Finally, the budget will have been set some time before the beginning of the current year and will need revisions in the light of changing trading conditions. Each month John is required to produce a quick forecast as to the likely spend by the end of the year. The 12 month forecast figures are therefore his own numbers which he submitted to the finance department just after the month end.

Every manager is also required to submit a short report outlining any reasons for significant underspends or overspends. This is then consolidated into a report on all the expense budgets for the organisation, which is then submitted to senior management. John's report for June is set out below:

Marketing Department Expense Budget: June
Actual expenses for the six months show a favourable variance against budget of £7,250. The main reason for the favourable variance is the three month delay earlier in the year in appointing the deputy marketing manager.

Training and conferences also show a favourable variance as most of the expenditure under this heading is used for the autumn sales conference.

Support staff salaries and travelling both show overspends against budget with smaller variances on telephone and other office expenses.

The forecast for the year shows a favourable variance against budget of £7,500.

Reviewing the budget

Put yourself into the role of a senior manager reviewing John's report. What additional questions might you ask?

There are a number of possible questions. The senior manager might well ask about the following:

> 1 **Marketing personnel salaries**
> The £10,000 favourable variance carries forward for the year so that the 12 months forecast is this amount less than budget. Are salaries really following the budget this closely or should the forecast for the year be amended?
>
> 2 **Support staff salaries**
> These are nine per cent up on budget for the first six months and the forecast for the year. Why?
>
> 3 **Travelling and telephone**
> For the first six months these items are up a third and a fifth respectively and yet are forecast to be back on budget for the 12 months as a whole. How can this be?
>
> 4 **Training and conferences**
> If the main expenditure takes place during the autumn, then this should be reflected in the phasing of the budget.

As always with financial information, the historic numbers tell a story about what has been happening in the business and the forecast numbers paint a picture of the future. The senior manager here is asking these questions:

◆ Have I received adequate explanations for what has happened in the past?

◆ Do I believe that the forecast is credible?

◆ Based on this information, are there decisions to be made?

In the first question on salaries, John is being quizzed as to how much thought he has put into the forecast. It is unlikely that the remuneration of everyone in the department is exactly as originally budgeted and if it has changed this should be reflected in the forecast figures.

The expense budget report does not provide the answers, but it does raise questions. The increase in support staff salaries may be due to the department being over the agreed head-count, cover for sickness or an authorised additional marketing exercise. Whatever the reason, this should be stated.

If no action is taken, we can expect expenditure to continue along the same trend. If travelling and telephone expenditure is well above budget for the first six months, our expectations are that it will continue to be above budget unless John does something. What is he intending to do to bring forecast expenditure back into line with the budget for the year?

Finally, taking the point made on the training and conference expenditure, you can see from the original report that the six months figures are exactly half the annual budget figures. This means no attempt has been made at phasing the budget – budgeting month by month according to how it is anticipated expenditure will actually take place.

Once the senior manager has discussed his questions with John, they will agree what action needs to be taken. Perhaps the original travelling budget was unrealistic and the company will live with the overspend, or perhaps everyone will be told to exercise tight control in this area until the end of the financial year.

Activity 7
The budgeting process

Objectives

In this activity you will be given an opportunity to reflect upon the operation of the budgeting process within your organisation. Specifically, by the end of this activity you will be able to:

◆ describe the budgeting process within your organisation

◆ evaluate the operation of the budgeting process

◆ identify areas with potential for improvement.

As we saw with the preparation of the sales forecast in Activity 6, the process by which the budget is put together will vary from organisation to organisation. However, the main stages in the process are likely to be those set out in Table 2.6.

2 Preparing and monitoring budgets

1	Provide details of budget assumptions and guidelines	These will cover the format of the budget and crucial underlying assumptions on economic indicators such as inflation and exchange rates, together with anticipated growth rates for relevant industrial sectors
2	Determine the factors that restrict output	An audit of production, human and other resources should be carried out to determine the limits on production
3	Preparation of the sales budget	This is the single most important budget. It is a function of the size of the market, the unit's share of that market and the selling price obtained
4	Initial preparation of various budgets	Once sales volume is known, the production and overhead departments can start putting together the budgets for their specific areas
5	Negotiation of budgets with superiors	It is human nature to want to have some slack in the system, whether this is a generous expenses budget or having plenty of stock to feed production
6	Co-ordination and review of budgets	It is usually the responsibility of financial management to make sure the budget is consistent, for example, that production is not making more than marketing say they can sell
7	Final acceptance of budgets	General managers of individual units may be asked to present and commit to their budgets at divisional and group levels
8	Ongoing review of budgets	The long timescales involved mean that budgets may need to be restated for changes in fundamental indicators of the organisation's position, for example, capital expenditure programmes may need to be cut if the organisation is generating insufficient cash in the face of an economic downturn

Table 2.6 *Stages in budget preparation*

Task

Compare these eight stages with the practice within your organisation.
You will need to obtain a copy of the budget procedures and talk to
your own manager and others involved in the process. Make a note of
your findings in the box provided.

Findings:

Feedback

The way the budget is prepared says much about the organisational and leadership style adopted by an organisation. It may be that, for reasons discussed further in the next activity, your management does not refer to budgets at all.

At the one extreme, in autocratic organisations a top-down approach to budget preparation may be adopted, with senior management passing down targets for those at lower levels to achieve. At the other extreme, the process may be seen as an opportunity for organisational learning, with all staff involved in the preparation of the budget and motivated to achieve the organisation's goals.

Where do your organisation's procedures for budget preparation fit between the two extremes? What does this say about your organisation's style of management?

Preparing financial plans

To run any organisation it is necessary to plan. We must say where we want to go and how we think we can best get there. There will be a financial dimension to nearly all the plans prepared by an organisation.

Figure 2.2 sets out a planning framework for an organisation.

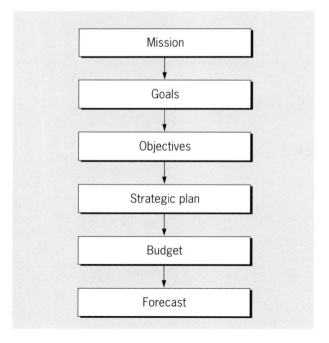

Figure 2.2 *Planning framework*

The mission statement sets out how the organisation views its primary purpose and is unlikely to contain any financial figures. The goals and objectives set out more specific aims. The strategic plan sets out the means by which the organisation intends to achieve its objectives. At the more detailed end of the planning process, the budgets and forecasts will still contain important narrative commentary but will also have detailed financial forecasts.

Financial planning in context

To illustrate each step, we will look at a small business which is refocusing to achieve greater profitability.

At each step, stand back and think of the processes within your own organisation.

Mission statement

Kay Hutchinson has been running a garden landscaping and maintenance business for some years. She has built up the business to the stage where she now employs two full-time members of staff. When getting the business started she accepted virtually any contract from any type of customer, often some distance away. She now feels she is in danger of becoming a 'busy fool' and wants to refocus the business.

She has thought carefully about what she wants to do and has decided the mission of her business will be to:

Provide householders, within her immediate geographical area, a personal landscaping service of a higher quality than that offered by larger competitors.

This is fine in that the mission statement sets out not only what she wants the business to do but also makes clear the business areas in which it does not operate, for example commercial contracts or a wide geographical area.

Goals

The goals of the business may be a mixture of the financial and non-financial.

Kay has decided the long-term goals of the new landscaping business will be:

1 To establish by word of mouth her company as a distinctive, quality provider of gardening services.

2 To generate at least 80 per cent of income from a list of regular clients to ensure continuity of income and minimise marketing effort.

45

3   To generate sufficient cash to meet the needs of the business and provide Kay personally with an income of £30,000 a year.

Kay could have taken another route to fulfilling her mission statement, for example high expenditure on advertising generating a series of high-margin, one-off contracts. Whatever route is taken, at the end of the day a business must generate sufficient cash to meet the requirements of all its stakeholders.

Objectives

Objectives are the shorter-term milestones in achieving the goals.

Kay's objectives for the next three years (Years 1–3) are:

1   To build up a client base of 120 regular local customers, with each customer being billed a minimum of £250 and on average £325.

2   To dispense with all contracts that involve working more than 15 miles from her home.

3   To generate profits of £25,000, £30,000 and then £35,000 in the next three years.

Strategy

More specific financial objectives have been set at this stage. The strategy is the plan which sets out the means by which Kay intends to achieve the objectives:

Kay Hutchinson Landscaping: corporate strategy for the next three years

1   Regular client base and increased average billings
   ◆   offer improved terms for annual contracts
   ◆   motivate staff to nurture larger clients
   ◆   increase charges for smaller clients
   ◆   advertising campaign in Year 1.

2   Reduce geographical coverage
   ◆   advise distant clients, over time, that the contracts will be terminated
   ◆   do not follow up new leads if further than 15 miles away.

3   Generate the target profits
   ◆   capital spend of £8,000 in Year 1 on new machinery to increase efficiency
   ◆   increase staff salaries by no more than the rate of inflation
   ◆   tight control of all costs.

As an appendix to the strategic plan there will probably be some key figures. For Kay these might be as shown in Table 2.7.

	Current year	Year 1	Forecast Year 2	Year 3
No. of clients	240	235	225	240
Average billing	£280	£300	£325	£325
	£	£	£	£
Sales	67,200	70,500	73,125	78,000
Profit/loss	20,000	20,000	25,000	30,000
Capital expenditure	3,000	8,000	4,000	4,000
Cash flow	20,000	16,000	26,000	32,000

Table 2.7 *Kay Hutchinson: strategic plan*

The strategic plan will still contain more narrative than numbers, but this schedule of key figures clearly gives a framework for the financial plans of the business. We can see that improvements in financial performance will come from increased billings per client and that the total number of clients will remain relatively static.

There will be a drop in cash flow in Year 1 as new machinery is bought. Any investor in the business must be kept fully informed as to why this drop in cash flow has taken place and the expectations of future improvement. Without this communication the investor may think the business is in trouble and withdraw support.

Budget and forecast

The final step in Kay's planning will be to produce more detailed plans for the coming year, see Table 2.8.

	Current year £	Budget Year 1 £
Sales	67,500	70,500
Salaries	36,000	37,000
Raw materials	2,500	2,500
Depreciation	3,000	4,000
Other costs	6,000	7,000
	47,500	50,500
Profit	20,000	20,000
Capital expenditure	3,000	8,000
Cash flow	20,000	16,000

Table 2.8 *Kay Hutchinson: budget for Year 1*

For the purpose of our illustration, we have just specified the costs. Supporting this statement would be schedules showing, for example, the salary costs of the two employees.

The key figures in the budget agree back to the strategic plan. This is important as the budget should be viewed as the first year of the strategic plan.

Finally, during Year 1 Kay may want to forecast her figures until the end of the year.

It is now the end of Year 1, and Kay has had a very good year:

◆ Smaller clients have simply accepted the increased charges and not gone to competitors as anticipated

◆ New clients are joining all the time, though most at £250 a year which means the business is not achieving its average billing of £325.

Kay's only real problem is finding staff in a buoyant local economy. One of her team has left to join a competitor and she is working all hours to keep on top of demand.

What should Kay do?

There is nothing wrong with making profits while you can; if business is good then make the most of it. Kay may have to pay very much more for staff in the future. She may have to increase charges yet further to a level unacceptable to her customers. It is possible that this may cause her to rethink her goals or even her mission statement.

As conditions have materially changed from the original forecast, Kay needs to think through her plans again and produce fresh financial forecasts. As long as she has her financial forecasts set up on a computer spreadsheet she will be able to model different possible futures and ask 'what-if?' questions.

Activity 8
Financial planning in context

Objective

This activity asks you to consider the advantages and disadvantages of the budgeting process. This activity will help you to:

◆ describe the reasons for the preparation of financial plans

◆ evaluate the contribution of financial planning to meeting the goals of your organisation

◆ recommend improvements to the financial planning process.

Task

There are six key reasons why organisations produce budgets. They are listed below. To what extent do you think your organisation acieves these benefits:

1 To aid the **planning** of annual operations:
   Major decisions will already have been made as part of the long-range, strategic planning effort but the budgetary process enables us to anticipate problems and think of better ways of doing things.

2 To **co-ordinate** the activities of the various parts of the organisation:
   Improving an organisation's results requires teamwork and the budgetary process can provide a useful framework for managers to work within, for example, pricing policy will require sales and finance to work together and effective stock control will require close liaison between production, purchasing and inventory managers.

3 To **communicate** plans to the various responsibility centre managers:
   The process of preparing the budget communicates information and makes the concerns and objectives of individual managers explicit.

4 To **motivate** managers to strive to achieve the organisational goals:
   To get the full benefits from budgeting, managers at all levels should be involved with the alignment of personal and organisational goals.

5 To **control** activities:
   The comparison of actual with budgeted figures enables management by exception – for managers to raise questions and concentrate action on those areas that deviate from budget.

6 To **evaluate** the performance of managers:
   Exactly how this is done, though, is subject to debate as it can be seen to be in conflict with the motivational and planning objectives.

Answer:

Feedback

Discuss your conclusions with your manager or colleagues. Consider the major constraints and opportunities that present themselves to your organisation.

Finally, reflect on how your personal objectives contribute to the organisation's overall objectives set out in the financial planning process. Can you see the precise way in which your work contributes to the financial success of your organisation?

◆ Recap

Assess the process for drawing up a sales forecast and critically appraise a sales forecast from your organisation

◆ A sales forecast is a financial estimate of what a business plans to sell in a future time period.

◆ Sales forecasts are based on past experience, statistical analysis and estimation, and consideration of various macroeconomic factors.

Explore the process for setting and managing expense budgets in your organisation

◆ Expense budgets refer to all expenditure in a business that is not directly associated with sales. Expense budgets provide a detailed estimate of what you plan to spend in a future time period.

◆ Top-down budgeting starts with senior management's expectations and goals and breaks these down into detail for the operating units. Bottom-up budgeting is more consultative, accumulating the detail of expected costs from each operating unit into an overall budget.

Evaluate the benefits and limitations of the financial planning process in your organisation

◆ As well as supporting the organisation's planning and control activities, a key benefit of budgeting is the communication of information around the organisation to support decision making. If done effectively, it is a motivational process that results in managers having greater ownership of their goals.

◆ Some organisations are moving away from traditional, detailed budgeting, arguing that budgets are often out of date before they are approved and the benefits do not justify the considerable effort required to create them.

►► More @

Broadbent, M. and Cullen, J. (2003) *Managing Financial Resources*, Butterworth-Heinemann

Owen, A. (2003) *Accounting for Business Studies*, Butterworth-Heinemann

The above general texts on financial management for managers provide further guidance and case studies on forecasting, budgeting and how to use financial information for decision making.

3   Pricing for profitability

> **The pricing decision is ... a complex mixture of strategic thought, operational planning, marketing and economic decision making by the supplier of the goods or service.**
>
> **Broadbent and Cullen (2003)**

You may think that deciding the selling price for products is a function of the marketing department, and indeed the prime responsibility does lie with them. However, the marketing department does not make the decision in isolation.

One of the basic questions to be asked about any product is, 'Are we making a profit on this product line?' Whilst companies have loss-leaders to attract custom, this can only ever be in exceptional circumstances if the business is to survive.

To maintain its profitability, an organisation needs to understand and take account of its costs when it makes pricing decisions. In this theme, you look at two techniques for allocating costs to products: full costing and marginal costing.

In this theme you will:

◆ **Learn how to make informed pricing decisions through using the full costing technique**

◆ **Practise preparing an estimate of costs using the full costing method and calculating a price**

◆ **Find out about marginal costing and identify situations where this is a useful technique.**

Pricing products

To know whether we are making a profit on an existing product or service we must know both:

◆ the price of the product – this should be readily available

◆ the cost of making that product or providing that service.

Providing information on cost is the central contribution financial managers make to decisions on product pricing.

One-product businesses

Determining the costs for a one-product business is relatively straightforward.

> Adam Kerr makes a famous cheese from the company's base in Dorset. The company produces 40,000 kilos a year and its annual costs are as follows:
>
> | | |
> |---|---|
> | Milk | £10,000 |
> | Other materials | £5,000 |
> | Wages | £60,000 |
> | Overheads | £30,000 |

The total costs of the business for the year are therefore £105,000 (10 + 5 + 60 + 30). If the company produces 40,000 kilos a year, then the cost of producing one kilo is £2.625.

Adam will sell the cheese at the highest price he can obtain over a period of time. But he now knows he must achieve a price of roughly £2.63 per kilo to cover costs.

In summary, for any business that only makes one product or provides one type of service, the cost per unit can be obtained by dividing total costs by the number of units.

Multi-product businesses

The situation becomes more complex when a number of products are produced or provided by a business.

> Adam informs you that although the company only produces cheese, he does in fact produce a range of three types and is worried about whether he is charging enough for the premium Vintage range.

What we need to do first for Adam is to allocate, as far as we are able, the costs to each of the three products. For the milk, the other direct materials and the direct labour we already know the information and all we need to do is set it out in an appropriate way. We show the breakdown in Table 3.1.

	Standard	Mature	Vintage	Total
Kilos produced	20,000	8,000	12,000	40,000
	£	£	£	£
Milk	4,400	2,000	3,600	10,000
Other materials	2,200	1,120	1,680	5,000
Direct labour	20,000	10,000	30,000	60,000
Overheads				30,000
Total costs				**105,000**

Table 3.1 *Adam Kerr: breakdown of product costs*

The milk, other materials and direct labour are known as direct costs because they are directly associated with providing the product. With most direct costs we are able to trace the costs to specific products. In the case of Adam, we could keep records over time to see how much milk and other materials went into the production runs for each of the three types of cheese.

With direct labour, we might observe the employees over a period of time to determine how much time it took to produce a batch of a particular product. From this information we could calculate the average time per kilo. For Adam the figures are set out in Table 3.2.

	Standard	Mature	Vintage	Total
Kilos produced	20,000	8,000	12,000	40,000
Wage cost per hour	£5	£5	£5	
Total labour hours	4,000	2,000	6,000	12,000
Direct labour cost	£20,000	£10,000	£30,000	£60,000
Direct labour hours per kilo	0.20	0.25	0.50	

Table 3.2 *Adam Kerr: summary of hours worked by product*

The summary shows that employees worked a total of 12,000 hours at a rate of £5 per hour during the last year. This agrees with the £60,000 (12,000 × £5) total cost for direct labour in Table 3.1. The 12,000 hours have been split between the three product lines on the basis of time records kept.

This enables us both to divide the total labour charge of £60,000 between the departments and also to calculate the average amount of time it takes to produce one kilo of each of the three products. We can see that it takes two and a half times as long to produce one kilo of Vintage as it does of Standard.

This still leaves us with the problem of how to allocate the overheads of £30,000 between the three departments. Unlike the direct costs, these **indirect costs** cannot be traced to individual products. We must find some way of allocating the costs which is broadly fair.

Calculating overhead recovery rates

The most common method used is to allocate the costs on the basis of the number of direct labour hours needed to produce one unit of product – in Adam's case a kilo of cheese. Thus for Adam we can produce the summary shown in Table 3.3.

	Standard	Mature	Vintage	Total
Total labour hours				12,000
Overheads				£30,000
Overheads recovered per direct labour hour (recovery rate)				£2.50
Kilos produced	20,000	8,000	12,000	40,000
Direct labour hours per kilo	0.20	0.25	0.50	
Overheads	£10,000	£5,000	£15,000	£30,000

Table 3.3 *Adam Kerr: recovery rate*

The recovery rate is the total overheads (£30,000) divided by the total number of direct labour hours (12,000) to give a recovery rate of £2.50 per hour. For every direct labour hour worked on producing a type of cheese, £2.50 is added to the costs in order to recover the total spend on overheads.

For example, overheads are allocated to the Standard product by multiplying the units (20,000) by the time taken to produce one unit (0.20 hours) by the recovery rate (£2.50). Check this now on a calculator for all three products.

What Table 3.3 shows is that the Vintage range bears 50 per cent (15,000 ÷ 30,000 × 100) of the costs of the overheads even though it only makes up 30 per cent (12,000 ÷ 40,000 × 100) of production by weight. This is because it takes longer to produce each kilo of this product.

We can now produce our breakdown of the total costs by product range, as shown in Table 3.4.

	Standard	Mature	Vintage	Total
Kilos produced	20,000	8,000	12,000	40,000
	£	£	£	£
Direct costs				
Milk	4,400	2,000	3,600	10,000
Other materials	2,200	1,120	1,680	5,000
Direct labour	20,000	10,000	30,000	60,000
	26,600	13,120	35,280	75,000
Overheads	10,000	5,000	15,000	30,000
Total costs	**36,600**	**18,120**	**50,280**	**105,000**

Table 3.4 *Adam Kerr: total costs by product range*

Interpreting the results

It is time to return to Adam's initial query. He is worried that he is selling the Vintage cheese at too low a price. He tells you that the Standard range sells for £2.50 a kilo, the Mature for £3.00 a kilo and the Vintage for £3.50 a kilo. This gives us the profit and loss account shown in Table 3.5.

	Standard	Mature	Vintage	Total
Kilos produced	20,000	8,000	12,000	40,000
Price per kilo	£2.50	£3.00	£3.50	
Profit and loss account	£	£	£	£
Sales	50,000	24,000	42,000	116,000
Total costs	36,600	18,120	50,280	105,000
Profit/(loss)	13,400	5,880	(8,280)	11,000

Table 3.5 *Adam Kerr: profit and loss account by product range*

The statement clearly shows that, as Adam fears, the Vintage range is making a loss.

Our simple example illustrates the principles involved in any costing system. Management will always need to weigh the cost of producing the information against the benefits in terms of improved decision making.

Adam has looked at our figures and has decided that he is going to stop producing Vintage cheese straight away. You might, however, want to caution Adam against any precipitate action.

1 The allocation of overheads to the different products is a matter of judgement, it is not a matter of hard fact. Allocating on the basis of direct labour hours is just a best attempt at making a reasonable allocation.

2 The overheads of £30,000 may not reduce significantly if production of Vintage is stopped. For example, it is unlikely the company could move to smaller premises without major upheaval. We will not do the detailed figures here, but stopping production of Vintage would greatly reduce, not increase, the overall profit.

3 Not all the effects are easily quantified in financial terms. The Vintage range may gain the company a lot of goodwill by being used in top restaurants and by television chefs. If this is the case, then this interest in the company may benefit sales of the other cheeses.

Adam would be much better off considering alternative courses of action. For instance, could he produce Vintage more efficiently or perhaps charge a higher price?

This section has looked at how to improve pricing decisions by allocating all the organisation's costs to the individual products produced. This is known as **full costing** and is useful because in the long run all the organisation's costs need to be built into the price if it is to make a profit.

Many organisations have very sophisticated systems for allocating costs to products. With increasing competition and tighter margins, organisations need to have reliable information on costs to feed into the pricing decision.

Activity 9
Preparing a quote

Objectives

In the following case study, there has been an enquiry from a customer and you are asked to produce a quote.

This activity will help you to:

◆ prepare an estimate of costs and possible price for a sales enquiry

◆ evaluate the basis upon which overheads are charged

◆ describe the contribution of the finance function to the pricing of products.

Case study

Ross Computer Services Ltd
Ross Computer Services Ltd supplies customised computer equipment. The financial plans for the next 12 months are as follows:

	£	£
Sales (billings to customers)		539,000
Direct materials	104,500	
Direct labour	88,000	(192,500)
Gross profit		346,500
Less expenses:		
Salaries	6,600	
Advertising	8,250	
Depreciation	75,900	
Administration	99,000	(189,750)
Operating profit		156,750
Less interest		22,000
Profit before tax		**£134,750**

Table 3.6 *Ross Computer Services Ltd: forecast profit and loss account for the 12 months to 31 December Year X*

A customer has asked the company to quote for a job. A first estimate of the direct costs for the job is as follows:

	£
Direct materials	11,000
Direct labour	9,900

Task

Based on this information, produce a possible quote for the customer. How far do you think it is sensible to use forecast financial information as a basis for pricing products?

Hot tip

You have been given the direct expenses. You need to decide on some means of allocating the overhead expenses and deciding on an appropriate mark-up.

Feedback

The workings for your quote should look something like those shown in Table 3.7.

Customer quotation number XXX	£	
Direct materials	11,000	Given
Direct labour	9,900	Given
Share of overheads (expenses)	?	
Share of interest charge	?	
Profit	?	
Quoted price	Sum of the above	

Table 3.7 *Preparing a quote – Stage 1*

The aim is to price all the company's products in such a way that if it made the planned £539,000 of sales it would make the planned profit of £134,750.

The direct labour costs for the job have been calculated to be £9,900 – this will have been worked out on the expected number of hours the job will take times the rates of pay for the different grades of labour used. Now, £9,900 is 11.25 per cent (£9,900 ÷ £88,000 x 100) of our total forecast wages bill for the year. It would seem sensible to allocate the same share of expenses and interest to the job, which gives us the figures shown in Table 3.8.

Customer quotation number XXX	£	
Direct materials	11,000	Given
Direct labour	9,900	Given
Share of overheads (expenses)	21,347	11.25% x £189,750
Share of interest charge	2,475	11.25% x £22,000
Profit	15,159	11.25% x £134,750
Quoted price	£59,881	Sum of the above

Table 3.8 *Preparing a quote – Stage 2*

This gives a suggested price for the job of £59,881. This calculation could be done in different ways with different answers. For instance, you could allocate a share of the expenses on the basis of the direct materials rather than the direct labour. This may be more appropriate in some cases, though generally the incurring of expenses is more directly related to the labour used than the materials.

Should Ross Computers then quote £59,881 for the job? Almost certainly not, if only because you would want to round your final figures to, say, £59,900. In practice, this calculation just broadly shows the sort of price the company must charge if it is to recover its overheads and make the planned profit. It may well be in this case that the sales manager thinks the customer will pay as much as £65,000 and, if that is the case, that is what the company should quote.

Pricing at the margin

We now look at situations where a company has been asked to supply a product at below its usual selling price. It may be that the company currently has spare capacity or has received an inquiry from an important potential customer. Analysing the situation involves using marginal costing techniques.

Marginal costing statements

Frank's Diner

Frank hires restaurant premises for lunchtime sessions where he sells food with an American theme at competitive prices. Business is satisfactory and he is planning for the next 12 months based on the following assumptions:

Days open per year	300 days
Capacity of the restaurant	80 customers per day
Forecast actual sales	50 customers per day
Selling price	£6.00 per meal
Materials costs	£2.50 per meal
Overheads per year	£45,000

Overhead expenditure is for the hire of the restaurant, staff wages, heating and lighting – in fact everything but the cost of the food, which varies directly with the number of meals sold.

The training manager of a local business comes in and asks if Frank can do lunch the next day for 20 people attending a training course at £4.00 per head. Another customer overhears the conversation and offers an annual contract to Frank to provide lunch every day for 20 of his employees at £4.00 per head.

What should Frank do? Should he accept either the training course or the annual contract, both or neither?

This is a common dilemma for business: where you have spare capacity, should you accept business at less than your standard prices?

The first thing we can do for Frank is draw up alternative profit forecasts for the coming year. First, we will calculate his original forecast as a 'base case', as shown in Table 3.9.

		£
Sales	300 × 50 × £6.00	90,000
Direct costs	300 × 50 × £2.50	37,500
Overheads		45,000
		82,500
Profit		7,500

Table 3.9 *Frank's Diner: original annual forecast*

Now we will show the effect on the profit of each of the two new business opportunities, see Table 3.10.

	Original £	Training course £	Annual contract £
Sales	90,000	80	24,000
Direct costs	37,500	50	15,000
Overheads	45,000	nil	nil
	82,500	50	15,000
Profit	7,500	30	9,000

Table 3.10 *Frank's Diner: revised annual forecast*

For the training course there is an £80 (20 × £4) increase in sales and a £50 (20 × £2.50) increase in direct costs. We know there is enough capacity to seat the additional diners as the restaurant holds 80 people and the additional 20 will bring the number of diners up to only 70. We are assuming that the existing kitchen and waiting staff can cope with the increase in numbers. On this assumption, taking on the additional diners will increase Frank's profit by £30 for the training course and it appears he should accept the business.

The figures for the annual contract look terrific, with profit increasing by over 100 per cent. However, they probably look a little too good and we will look at the annual contract again later in this section.

We can do the same analysis setting out our figures in the form of a marginal costing statement, see Table 3.11. Here we say that the selling price is £6.00, the variable cost £2.50 and so the contribution each meal sold makes towards covering the overheads is £3.50.

	Total	Per unit
Unit sales	15,000	
	£	£
Sales	90,000	6.00
Variable costs	37,500	2.50
Contribution	52,500	3.50
Fixed costs	45,000	
Profit	**7,500**	

Table 3.11 *Frank's Diner: marginal costing statement*

Marginal costing statements analyse costs between those which vary directly with the number of units sold and those which remain the same however little or much is sold. In the case of Frank's Diner this is relatively straightforward as all his costs are fixed except for the food purchased. We can say that each meal sold makes a contribution of £3.50 towards meeting Frank's fixed costs.

Break-even analysis

This type of analysis enables us to answer other important questions, for example, how many meals will Frank have to sell next year to break even? By 'break even' we mean make neither a profit nor a loss. The answer is his fixed costs divided by the contribution each unit makes:

£45,000 ÷ £3.50 = 12,857 meals

We say that the break-even point is 12,857 meals. To prove this is so, we will revise the marginal costing statement for this number of meals, see Table 3.12.

	Total	Per unit
Unit sales	12,857	
	£	£
Sales	77,142	6.00
Variable costs	32,142	2.50
Contribution	45,000	3.50
Fixed costs	45,000	
Profit	**nil**	

Table 3.12 *Frank's Diner: revised marginal costing statement*

Margin of safety

In addition to the break-even point, we might want to know what this tells us about our margin of safety – by how much does our sales forecast have to be wrong before we start showing a loss?

In Frank's case this is given by:

15,000 units (the original forecast) minus 12,857 (the break-even point)

This gives us a margin of safety of 2,143 meals or £12,858 (£6.00 × 2,143) in terms of sales.

'What-if?' questions

Marginal costing statements are useful for showing us the profit at any level of activity. The use of spreadsheets is particularly useful for asking quick 'what-if?' questions. For example, what if Frank dropped his selling price from £6 to £5 and this increased the number of meals sold from 15,000 to 17,000? Restating our forecast marginal costing statement gives us the result shown in Table 3.13.

	Total	Per unit
Unit sales	17,000	
	£	£
Sales	85,000	5.00
Variable costs	42,500	2.50
Contribution	42,500	2.50
Fixed costs	45,000	
Profit/(loss)	(2,500)	

Table 3.13 *Frank's Diner: marginal costing statement with £5 selling price*

The what-if analysis shows that our original profit of £7,500 would turn into a loss of £2,500 under this proposal and that it is best rejected.

Finally, we will return to the proposal we met at the beginning of this section. A customer has offered an annual contract of 20 meals a day at £4 per meal. Should Frank accept the offer? Well, 20 meals a day for 300 days is an extra 6,000 meals a year, so we could revise our forecast as shown in Table 3.14.

	Original forecast	Annual contract	Total
Unit sales	15,000	6,000	21,000
	£	£	£
Sales	90,000	24,000	114,000
Direct costs	37,500	15,000	52,500
Overheads	45,000	0	45,000
	82,500	15,000	97,500
Profit	7,500	9,000	16,500

Table 3.14 *Frank's Diner: profit forecast with additional annual contract*

Here the forecast shows a healthy increase in profit from £7,500 to £16,500. In fact this is suspiciously healthy – *why do you think this forecast might not be realistic?*

Whilst the restaurant may be able to cater for the additional 20 people from the training course for one day, it is unlikely that it could cater for an extra 20 people (over a third of the existing customers) every day on the annual contract without employing extra kitchen staff and waiters – so the fixed costs will increase.

This shows one of the limitations of marginal costing: it only holds true for a range of activity; outside this range fixed costs will vary. There are other limitations too. The technique is very difficult to apply where an organisation makes more than one product. Also, it assumes all costs are either fixed or perfectly variable, but many costs are semi-variable; even with raw materials, beyond a certain level bulk discounts may be available.

The technique has its uses, particularly when evaluating new product launches. It has the advantage that it is readily understandable by everyone involved and can be used to model a range of alternatives.

Activity 10
Cost–volume–profit

Objectives

Marginal costing, or the relationship between cost, volume and profit, is the subject of this activity. It will help you to:

◆ describe situations where cost–volume analysis is useful

◆ evaluate the usefulness of the techniques for your organisation.

Task

Investigate how prices are determined within your organisation and how useful marginal costing techniques are to the operation of your business.

For one or two products, try to find out:

◆ who took the decision on the price to be charged

◆ what information was available on which to base the decision

◆ what contribution, if any, the finance function made to the decision.

Use the chart below to record your findings.

Product	Who took the pricing decision	Information that was available	Contribution of finance function

Reflect upon the applicability of what you have learned about pricing and cost allocation to the practices within your organisation.

Feedback

The way prices are fixed will vary greatly between businesses.

There are a number of limitations to marginal costing techniques, which you may have found during your investigation. These limitations are explained here:

- The assumption that volume is the only factor that will cause costs and revenues to change. If you have ever studied economics you will remember about the elasticity of demand where lower prices generate higher volumes of sales. On the supply side, there may be economies of scale as volume increases.

- Marginal costing really requires a single product or a constant sales mix. In practice, the break-even point is not a unique number but varies depending on the composition of the sales mix.

- Fixed costs only remain fixed for a range of production. For instance, beyond a certain level of output it will be necessary to buy new plant or increase administrative and sales support. The method therefore works best within a short-term period since in the long term all costs are variable.

- Finally, even within the short term, it may be very difficult to divide costs into their fixed and variable elements.

◆ Recap

Learn how to make informed pricing decisions through using the full costing technique

- A direct cost is one which directly relates to whatever is being costed. An indirect cost is one that only partly relates to whatever is being costed.

- Indirect costs (overheads) must be reflected in calculating the total cost of a product or service and in its pricing. This is known as full costing.

Practise preparing an estimate of costs using the full costing method and calculating a possible price

- When setting prices, the business first needs to apportion its indirect costs between the various products or services it produces. It then needs to apply a mark-up to calculate the selling price.

Find out about marginal costing and identify situations where this is a useful technique

◆ Marginal costing assists short-term decision making by calculating the contribution each unit makes towards the fixed costs of the business. It is calculated as:

Selling price – variable cost = contribution.

◆ Marginal costing is appropriate for making decisions about:

  – cost–volume–profit relationships

  – acceptance of a special order

  – what-if scenarios, for example whether to make components in-house or to buy them in.

 **More @**

Broadbent, M. and Cullen, J. (2003) *Managing Financial Resources,* Butterworth-Heinemann

Owen, A. (2003) *Accounting for Business Studies,* Butterworth-Heinemann

Both the above texts extend the coverage provided in this theme, providing accessible information on costing and pricing for non-financial managers.

BetterManagement.com – www.bettermanagement.com
Try this business management resource for articles and white papers on wide-ranging financial topics.

Reviewing financial performance

It is a feature of financial statements that they contain an awful lot of numbers. This theme provides you with some tools to help you separate the wood from the trees and draw out the key questions to be asked. Without this toolkit it is very difficult to start any analysis or evaluation of financial performance.

You will be introduced to a range of performance indicators that you can use to evaluate financial performance, in particular the use of key financial ratios. Financial ratios express one piece of financial information (for example profit) in terms of another (for example total assets). The result is then compared with the equivalent result for another time period or organisation to identify trends in financial performance. You will look at the some of the financial ratios that are used to analyse profitability, working capital, gearing and investment.

In this theme you will:

◆ **Explore techniques for monitoring trends in financial performance**

◆ **Find out how to analyse the profitability of an organisation using the major profitability ratios**

◆ **Describe what is meant by capital investment and appraise the financial statement supporting an investment proposal**

◆ **Discover the components of and main ways of controlling working capital**

◆ **Distinguish between the three main sources of finance for a business and explore what is meant by gearing.**

Making numbers meaningful

The statement shown in Table 4.1 is for Omega Components which imports components for domestic appliance manufacturers. It shows last year's actual results (Year 1), the latest forecast to the end of the current year (Year 2) and the original budget for the current year.

	Year 1 Actual £	Year 2 Forecast £	Year 2 Budget £
Sales	14,000	16,000	15,000
Cost of sales	7,700	9,280	8,250
Gross profit	6,300	6,720	6,750
Overheads			
Salaries	2,200	2,400	2,300
Marketing costs	1,500	1,800	1,800
Administration costs	1,000	1,300	1,000
Other costs	700	600	700
	5,400	6,100	5,800
Profit	900	620	950

Table 4.1 *Omega Components: profit and loss accounts*

Take a few minutes to look at this statement and answer the question: *How is Omega doing?*

Well, clearly the profit forecast for the year at £620 is below the budget at £950, which stands above last year's actual profit of £900. However, forecast sales are above budget and last year's figure of £14,000, whilst the forecast gross profit at £6,720 is also above last year's actual which is etc. etc. etc.

This sort of reporting on what is 'up' and 'down' really gets you nowhere and when written in financial reports is guaranteed to produce glazed eyes.

If we were able to say 'Forecast profit at £620 is 31 per cent down on the previous year because...', this would be a firmer starting point.

Common size analysis

In fact, to make sense of profit and loss statements at all we really have to use percentages. As a first step, we have produced a common size analysis where all the figures have been restated as a percentage of sales. See Table 4.2.

	Year 1 Actual %	Year 2 Forecast %	Year 2 Budget %
Sales	100	100	100
Cost of sales	55	58	55
Gross profit	45	42	45
Overheads			
Salaries	16	15	15
Marketing costs	11	11	12
Administration costs	7	8	7
Other costs	5	4	5
	39	38	39
Profit	6	4	6

Table 4.2 *Omega Components: common size analysis*

Take a few moments to make sure you understand how this statement has been calculated. Each actual figure has been divided by the sales and then expressed as a percentage. For instance, the forecast marketing costs of £1,800 divided by the sales of £16,000 gives 0.1125, which multiplied by 100 gives 11 per cent. This sort of calculation can be done in a few seconds in a spreadsheet.

Spreadsheets are the modern manager's equivalent of 'back of the envelope' calculations but much more powerful. If you have a basic understanding of spreadsheets, then Table 4.1 can be viewed as an 'input' area – all the figures except the totals are physically typed in. Table 4.2 should just contain formulas for the percentage calculation as set out in the previous paragraph – with copy and paste functions, you only need to type in the formulas for one column.

We are now ready to do what-if analysis. *What if* our forecast sales are £500 more than expected? *What if* our costs of sales are £200 less than expected? *What if* administration costs turn out to be on budget after all? *What if* ... etc. All these changes can be modelled by simply changing the numbers in the input area and the common size analysis will be recalculated automatically.

Gross profit margin

Gross profit for this type of business represents sales less the cost of goods bought in. Expressed as a percentage of sales it gives the gross profit margin, which is one of the key indicators for this type of business. The gross profit margin at Omega Components for last year end budget is 45 per cent (6,300 ÷ 14,000 × 100) against a forecast of 42 per cent. This is a very significant movement which is not apparent from looking at the raw figures.

The advantage of this type of statement is that it takes out the effect of variations in the level of sales. In the case of Omega, if the general manager is asked why forecast cost of sales at £9,280 was above budget she could quite reasonably reply, 'Well of course it is, our sales are higher than budget and this would be impossible without more purchases'. What she is saying is true, but not useful.

If, however, the manager is asked why the gross profit margin has dropped from 45 per cent to 42 per cent, then her answer must address one of three possibilities:

◆ *Either* there has been an increase in prices charged by suppliers which has not been passed on to the customer, *or*

◆ Supplier prices have remained steady, but the amount charged to customers has been reduced, *or*

◆ The company is operating less efficiently so that more costs are incurred for each unit of output.

Variance analysis

Common size analysis is less useful for evaluating movements in individual overheads. The common size analysis in Table 4.2 shows overheads falling as a percentage of sales from 39 per cent to 38 per cent – on the face of it a positive trend. However, the forecast overheads are expressed as a percentage of a buoyant sales figure and the actual rise is £700 (£6,100 – £5,400) or 13 per cent (£700 ÷ £5,400 × 100) on last year.

A better alternative is to analyse the figures to show the differences (variances) between the three columns, as shown in Table 4.3.

Table 4.3 *Omega Components: profit and loss account showing variance*

	Year 2 Forecast £	Year 2 Budget £	Year 2 Variance £	Year 1 Actual £
Sales	16,000	15,000	1,000	14,000
Cost of sales	9,280	8,250	(1,030)	7,700
Gross profit	6,720	6,750	(30)	6,300
Overheads				
Salaries	2,400	2,300	(100)	2,200
Marketing costs	1,800	1,800	nil	1,500
Administration costs	1,300	1,000	(300)	1,000
Other costs	600	700	100	700
	6,100	5,800	(300)	5,400
Profit	620	950	(330)	900

In Table 4.3 the profit and loss account has been restated into a format which is similar to that used for internal reporting within many organisations. The focus for management action is on the forecast for the current year, so this column has been placed first. The budget for the second year are the figures against which we measure, so this is placed next.

To save time subtracting forecast from budget figures, this has been done in the third column. The actual figures for last year are important, first because they are fact as opposed to management projections, and secondly because it is against last year's actual figures that stakeholders, including external investors, will largely judge an organisation's performance.

This statement shows overspends on all overhead items except for marketing costs. Looking across at the actual figures you can see a substantial increase of £400 (£5,800 – £5,400) over the previous year's overheads was already in the budget. A further increase above this is very worrying.

We are now in a position to ask the management of Omega Components some searching questions. *What questions would you ask?*

Not surprisingly, the financial analysis is raising questions rather than providing answers. There are many questions that could be asked – here are a selection:

◆ Sales are forecast to be seven per cent (1,000 ÷ 15,000 × 100) up on budget and 14 per cent (2,000 ÷ 14,000 × 100) up on last year. How much of this is due to an increase in the volume of sales and how much due to price increases? Are we doing better or worse than our competitors?

◆ The gross profit margin is forecast to be only 42 per cent against 45 per cent last year. This may suggest that volume increases have been bought at the expense of lower selling prices but this will need to be confirmed. If the decrease is due to higher raw material costs, why have we not been able to pass these on to our customers in the form of higher prices?

◆ Why are administration costs forecast to be some £300 above budget and last year's figure? A detailed breakdown is required of all expenditure under this heading.

◆ Overall, overheads are showing a 13 per cent (700 ÷ 5,400 × 100) increase over last year. This requires explanation. If sales dropped off, we would need to make radical cuts in this level of overheads in order to remain in profit.

Activity 11
Management accounts

Objectives

Activity 1 asked you to obtain copies of your organisation's internal financial reports. Using what you have learned so far in this book, use this activity to look more closely at the management accounts produced by your business.

This activity will help you to:

◆ analyse the monthly reporting within your organisation

◆ construct a list of the main sources of financial information

◆ evaluate how the reporting meets the business needs.

Task

Building on your work in Activity 1, ask if you can see the different financial reports that are produced on a monthly basis. Specifically, find out the following:

Feedback

Internal reporting practices vary greatly between organisations, although the basic financial statements produced are nearly always the same.

What financial statements and reports are produced

How the information is set out, for instance, are comparisons made with budget/last year?

The sources of the information for the monthly accounts

You will expect to see a profit and loss account, cash flow statement and balance sheet produced for your business unit. The only exception to this is if your unit only has responsibility for sales or profit and not for the assets employed in the business; this may be the case if it is primarily a sales unit operating on behalf of other group companies.

It is likely that there will be pages of supplementary information and analysis. The content will depend on the nature of your business but is likely to include sales analysis and summaries of capital expenditure.

The actual results for the month and for the year-to-date will probably be compared with the budget figures. In addition there may be budget and forecast figures for the year together with prior-year comparisons.

It is easy to think of the management accounts as something the accounts department produces but in practice they are dependent upon the information fed into them by the various departments. This will be particularly true for any forecast figures which are built up from the sales forecast. Find out the sources of information for your organisation's monthly management accounts.

Finally, if you work for a group of companies, the format of the management accounts may be laid down by head office. This is necessary for the review of accounts at divisional or group level. If this is the case, ask how much managers feel this group format serves the needs of your own unit or whether the unit produces its own information in addition to meeting group requirements.

Making a return on capital employed

This section focuses upon the key ratios used to investigate the return being achieved on the investment made (or capital employed) in the business.

Competing for investment

Stephen will be retiring in five years' time and is reviewing his investments.

In addition to his company pension, he has built up investments in shares and savings accounts worth £120,000. The current income from the investments is about £8,400 per year. Stephen is not happy that this will be enough and feels that £10,000 income per year is needed to meet his requirements.

What options are open to Stephen?

There are a great number of possible alternative actions he could take in terms of buying and selling investments. But his possible actions boil down to two main alternatives:

- save more, increasing the amount he has invested
- seek a higher return on the money he has already invested.

His current rate of return is seven per cent per annum (8,400 ÷ £120,000 × 100). So, if he wants an income of £10,000 per year, at seven per cent he must invest around £143,000 (£10,000 ÷ 0.07).

If he is able, he would much prefer to get a higher return and have more money to spend. For £10,000 income from savings of £120,000 he would need a return of 8.3 per cent per year.

Your company is competing with other companies for Stephen's money. If you can offer Stephen a higher return, then he will invest with you. This will enable your company to purchase the assets it needs to survive and grow. You will need to ensure that you generate sufficient return from your assets to actually pay Stephen the money you have promised him.

Return on capital employed (ROCE)

To get our bearings, consider Table 4.4, which shows actual figures for Squishies Ltd.

Profit and loss account for Year 1	£	Balance sheet as at 31 December, Year 1	£
Sales	800,000	Fixed assets	300,000
Cost of sales	350,000		
		Working capital	
Gross profit	450,000	Stock	80,000
		Debtors	140,000
Expenses		Bank	30,000
Selling expenses	220,000	Less: Creditors	50,000
Distribution	50,000		
Administration	60,000		200,000
	330,000		500,000
Net profit	120,000		
		Funded by	
		Shareholders' funds	100,000
		Borrowings	400,000
			500,000
Net profit margin	15%		
Gross profit margin	56%		
Return on capital employed	24%		
Asset turnover (times)	1.60		

Table 4.4 *Squishies Ltd: financial statements Year 1*

Squishies makes soft ice cream and is a profitable company. In Year 1 it made a net profit of £120,000 on sales of £800,000, a net profit margin of 15 per cent (120,000 ÷ 800,000 × 100).

To generate these sales it required an investment of £300,000 in long-term fixed assets and £200,000 in current assets (working capital – the breakdown shown in the box), giving a balance sheet value for assets employed in the business of £500,000. So, we can say that the assets were 'turned over' 1.6 times (800,000 ÷ 500,000) during the year. This gives us an indicator of how much money needs to be invested to generate a given level of sales. In the case of Squishies, it needs to invest £1 in assets to generate £1.60 worth of sales each year.

The company is making a return of £120,000 on the £500,000 invested in the business. This is known as **return on capital employed** (ROCE) and for Squishies Ltd comes to 24 per cent (120,000 ÷ 500,000 × 100). In order to attract the money of investors such as Stephen, it needs to make this return as high as possible.

The 24 per cent return on capital employed is equal to the net profit margin of 15 per cent times the asset turnover of 1.6. For the mathematically minded this is because:

Return on capital employed %
(Net profit ÷ Capital employed × 100) =

$$\frac{\text{Net profit margin %}}{\text{(Net profit ÷ Sales × 100)}} \times \frac{\text{Asset turnover}}{\text{(Sales ÷ Capital employed)}}$$

For the less mathematically inclined, it is the practical consequences that matter.

If we want to increase our return on capital employed, and naturally we do, there are only two areas we can address, either separately or at the same time:

1 We can take action to increase our profit margin – make more money on each £1 of sales we make.

2 We can make our assets work harder – generate more sales for each £1 of assets we have employed in the business.

Improving profitability

We will conclude this section by looking at the first of these areas. There are several possible ways of improving profitability, and we will try to summarise possible approaches here.

Table 4.5 shows the actual profit and loss account for Year 1 shown earlier in Table 4.4. Management is now considering its options for Year 2.

	Year 1 – Actual £	Year 2 – Option 1 £	Year 2 – Option 2 £
Sales	800,000	840,000	840,000
Cost of sales	350,000	367,500	344,400
Gross profit	450,000	472,500	495,600
Expenses			
Selling expenses	220,000	250,000	250,000
Distribution	50,000	50,000	50,000
Administration	60,000	60,000	60,000
	330,000	360,000	360,000
Net profit	120,000	112,500	135,600
Capital employed	500,000	500,000	500,000
Net profit margin	15%	13%	16%
Gross profit margin	56%	56%	59%
Return on capital employed	24%	23%	27%
Asset turnover (times)	1.6	1.7	1.7

Table 4.5 *Squishies Ltd: possible profit and loss accounts in Year 2*

The marketing manager considers that the Squishies brand needs rejuvenating and that an additional spend of £30,000 on advertising is essential. With this increase in spending will come additional sales volume of five per cent in Year 2 in addition to the long-term benefits for the brand.

The 'Option 1' column in Table 4.5 shows the effect of these two changes on the profit and loss account and on key ratios. The effect is to reduce the net profit margin as the increased gross profit is insufficient to cover the increase in overheads.

To put this another way, you will recall that:

- the cost of sales is the cost of raw materials and other costs directly associated with producing the product
- gross profit is sales less these costs of sales.

The five per cent increase in sales gives us £40,000 of increased sales which at a gross profit margin of 56 per cent gives us additional gross profit of £22,500. We are spending an additional £30,000 on advertising so we can expect, as the figures show, a drop in net profit of £7,500.

Management considers this drop in profit to be unacceptable. However, the production director says that the commodity markets in which it buys its raw materials are forecast to weaken in Year 2 and there may be the opportunity to reduce the cost of goods bought in. The higher sales levels will also present more opportunities for bulk purchase discounts.

Currently, with a gross profit margin of 56 per cent, cost of sales represents 44 per cent of sales value. The production director thinks this figure could be reduced to 41 per cent of sales, increasing the gross profit margin to 59 per cent. 'Option 2' in Table 4.5 shows how this change produces a substantial increase in profits to £135,600.

In summary, there are a number of areas for possible management action to improve profitability, namely:

- increase sales volume
- increase the gross margin, either:
    - by increasing selling price without increasing cost of sales, or
    - decreasing cost of sales without reducing the selling price
- decrease overheads.

As even our very simple example suggests, the process of financial planning is much more dynamic than this simple listing implies, with suggested action plans affecting several profit and loss account headings at the same time.

Activity 12
Return on capital employed

Objectives

This activity will help you to:

◆ compare the current performance with comparative data

◆ produce key return on capital employed ratios

◆ evaluate the financial results.

Case study

Wheetman plc

The following financial statements for Wheetman plc are a slightly simplified set of published accounts; published accounts are discussed later in this book. Wheetman plc is an engineering firm which developed a new range of products in 2000; these were introduced in 2001 and now account for some 40 per cent of turnover. See Tables 4.6 and 4.7.

(The analysis of Wheetman's accounts is continued in Activities 13 and 14.)

	2001 £000	2000 £000
Turnover	11,205	7,003
Cost of sales	5,809	3,748
Gross profit	5,396	3,255
Operating expenses	3,087	2,205
Profit before interest	2,309	1,050
Interest payable	456	216
Profit before tax	1,853	834
Taxation	390	210
Profit after tax	1,463	624
Dividends	400	300
Retained profit	1,063	324
Retained profit brought forward	685	361
Retained profit carried forward	1,748	685

Table 4.6 *Wheetman plc: profit and loss account for the year ended 31 March 2001*

	2001 £000	2000 £000
Fixed assets	8,235	4,300
Current assets		
Stocks	2,410	1,209
Trade debtors	1,372	807
Other debtors	201	134
Cash	4	28
	3,987	2,178
Current liabilities		
Trade creditors	1,306	607
Other creditors	201	124
Taxation	390	210
Dividends	400	300
Overdraft	1,625	–
	(3,922)	(1,241)
Net current assets	65	937
Total net assets	8,300	5,237
Bank loan	3,800	1,800
	4,500	3,437
Share capital	1,800	1,800
Capital reserve	952	952
Retained profits	1,748	685
	4,500	3,437

Table 4.7 *Wheetman plc: balance sheet as at 31 March 2001*

The headings used in the tables are expanded from those used previously in our examples and correspond more closely to those used in UK published accounts.

In Table 4.7, debtors and creditors are split between 'trade' and 'other'.

'Trade' refers to the day-to-day transactions with the company's customers and suppliers. 'Other' items might include things such as the amounts owed by staff in respect of moving expenses or amounts owed to the supplier of fixed assets. The creditor amounts for taxation and dividends simply refer to the amount owing at the balance sheet date to the government tax authorities and the company's shareholders respectively.

Compared with the accounts for Squishies Ltd used in the previous section, the profit and loss account for Wheetman plc, Table 4.6, shows how the profit from operations has been used. In 2001, £456,000 has been paid in interest to the suppliers of loans, £390,000 in taxation to the government and £400,000 in dividends to the shareholders. Out of the profit before interest (also known as operating profit) of £2,309,000 this leaves £1,063,000 left in the business to fund future growth.

We will take a further look at the balance sheet in the final activity.

Task

Calculate the following ratios for both 2001 and 2000, then answer the question that follows.

Return on capital employed

Net profit margin

Asset turnover

When calculating the ratios, use the 'Profit before interest' and 'Total net asset' figures.

What do these three ratios tell us about the company's performance in 2001 compared with the previous year?

Feedback

The calculation of the ratios is given in Table 4.8.

		2001	*2000*
Return on capital employed	Profit before interest ÷ Total net assets x 100	2,309 ÷ 8,300 x 100 = 27.8%	1,050 ÷ 5,237 x 100 = 20.0%
Profit margin	Profit before interest ÷ Sales x 100	2,309 ÷ 11,205 x 100 = 20.6%	1,050 ÷ 7,003 x 100 = 15.0%
Asset turnover	Sales ÷ Total net assets	11,205 ÷ 8,300 = 1.35	7,003 ÷ 5,237 = 1.34

Table 4.8 *Calculation of ratios*

Look at each ratio in turn and ask yourself whether the change from 2000 to 2001 is 'good' or 'bad'.

The return on capital employed has increased from 20 per cent to over 27 per cent; this must be good as the company's aim is to maximise the return it makes on the assets employed in the business.

Profit margin has increased from 15.0 per cent to 20.6 per cent, which again must be good as it means the company is making more profit for each £1 of sales that it makes.

Asset turnover has remained approximately the same at 1.35. This tells us that to generate each £1 of sales requires the same investment in assets in 2001 as in the previous year.

So in conclusion, we can report that Wheetman plc's return on capital employed has improved by 7.8 per cent to 27.8 per cent due to an increased profit margin, with the efficiency with which assets are utilised remaining unchanged.

Because profit margin multiplied by asset turnover equals return on capital employed, we can make this statement with certainty. What we need to investigate further is what has given rise to the increase in profit margin and whether the company's different types of assets are all being worked with the same efficiency.

Activity 13
Analysing profitability

Objectives

This activity builds upon the analysis of Wheetman plc's accounts which was started in Activity 12.

We saw in Activity 12 that Wheetman plc increased its profit margin to 20.6 per cent. This activity asks you to look more closely at the reasons behind this increase.

Use this activity to:

◆ compare current profit performance with comparative data

◆ produce key profit and loss account ratios and analysis

◆ evaluate the financial results.

The profit and loss account for Wheetman plc, shown in Activity 12, is repeated in Table 4.9.

	2001 £000	2000 £000
Turnover	11,205	7,003
Cost of sales	5,809	3,748
Gross profit	5,396	3,255
Operating expenses	3,087	2,205
Profit before interest	2,309	1,050
Interest payable	456	216
Profit before tax	1,853	834
Taxation	390	210
Profit after tax	1,463	624
Dividends	400	300
Retained profit	1,063	324
Retained profit brought forward	685	361
Retained profit carried forward	1,748	685

Table 4.9 *Wheetman plc: profit and loss account for the year ended 31 March 2001*

The profit left after the government has taken its share in the form of taxation is available for distribution (payment) to shareholders in the form of a dividend. Companies will not want to pay out all this profit as a dividend because to grow the company they need to retain profits in the business. Any profit left over is retained in the business. The profit retained for the current year is added to the retained profit brought forward from previous years, to give the retained profit carried forward to the next year.

Business units which form part of a larger group of companies will be funded by head office and will not have their own shareholders nor responsibility for agreeing their tax liabilities. Local business unit managers only really have control over profit down to the profit before taxation line and it is this that we will concentrate on here.

One useful way of analysing the profit and loss account is to produce a common size analysis which restates all figures as a percentage of sales. This statement together with a column showing the percentage year-on-year movement will provide most of the analysis needed to start evaluating the results. A common size analysis for Wheetman plc is produced in Table 4.10.

	2001 £000	%	2000 £000	%	Movement %
Turnover	11,205	100.0	7,003	100.0	60.0
Cost of sales	5,809	51.8	3,748	53.5	55.0
Gross profit	5,396	48.2	3,255	46.5	65.8
Operating expenses	3,087	27.6	2,205	31.5	40.0
Profit before interest	2,309	20.6	1,050	15.0	119.9
Interest payable	456	4.1	216	3.1	111.1
Profit before tax	1,853	16.5	834	11.9	122.2

Table 4.10 *Wheetman plc: common size analysis*

Task

1 Use your calculator to check that you understand how all the numbers in this analysis are derived.

2 Your main task is then to produce a list of questions for local management based on your interpretation of these numbers.

Feedback

This analysis cannot produce answers but it can produce some searching questions.

All the analysis of profitability takes place against a background of a 60 per cent increase in turnover. This is an excellent result and local management should be congratulated. We might ask various questions about turnover:

◆ What are the main factors that gave rise to this increase?

◆ How did your competitors perform?

◆ Is this increased level of performance sustainable?

◆ Did the company manage to maintain/increase prices?

The gross profit margin has increased from 46.5 per cent to 48.2 per cent. Movements at the gross profit level need to be monitored closely as relatively small movements here have major influences lower down the profit and loss account. We might ask:

◆ Was the increase in the gross profit margin due to raising selling prices or reduced supplier costs, or a mixture of the two?

Operating expenses as a percentage of sales have reduced from 31.5 per cent to 27.6 per cent and on the face of it this is good. However, they have increased over the previous year by 40 per cent – it is only because sales are so buoyant that the figures look so good. Remember that operating expenses are mainly fixed expenses such as administration, selling and distribution costs. If sales were to turn down in Year 3, Wheetman plc would be in all sorts of trouble and might have to take drastic action to reduce its overheads. We might ask local management:

◆ Please provide a detailed breakdown of the operating expenses showing exactly where the increases have taken place.

◆ What were the reasons for the increases in the different operating expenses?

◆ Can these increases be justified or should the company be taking steps to reduce its cost base?

Finally, interest charges have more than doubled from £216 to £456 and this is worrying. We will return to this in the final activity, but for the moment we might ask:

How much, if any, of the increased interest charge is due to general increases in interest rates and how much is due to increased borrowings?

Long-term capital investment

The sort of investments we are thinking of in this section may be in plant and equipment for a manufacturing concern, distribution facilities for a service company or new offices. The investment will appear in the balance sheet under the heading 'fixed assets'.

It is a feature of this type of investment that it is for the long term and very difficult to reverse. For this reason, good investment decisions will lay the foundation for continuing success, whilst organisations may have to live with the adverse effects of bad decisions for many years.

Preparing the cash flow forecast

In the last section we introduced Squishies Ltd, a profitable company that makes ice cream. To recap, the company's financial position in Year 1 was as shown in Table 4.11.

Profit and loss account for Year 1	£	Balance sheet as at 31 December, Year 1	£
Sales	800,000	Fixed assets	300,000
Cost of sales	350,000		
Gross profit	450,000	Working capital	
		Stock	80,000
		Debtors	140,000
Expenses		Bank	30,000
Selling expenses	220,000	Less: Creditors	50,000
Distribution	50,000		
Administration	60,000		200,000
	330,000		**500,000**
		Funded by	
		Shareholders' funds	100,000
Net profit	120,000	Borrowings	400,000
			500,000
Net profit margin	15%		
Gross profit margin	56%		
Return on capital employed	24%		
Asset turnover (times)	1.60		

Table 4.11 *Squishies Ltd: financial statements, Year 1*

Squishies Ltd currently operates only in the UK where the market is static but there is the exciting possibility of setting up a parallel operation in France. The company has been approached with the offer of an existing production facility by another company withdrawing from the market. The financial manager has been asked to produce a cash flow forecast for the first year of operation in France and has come up with the numbers shown in Table 4.12.

Cash flow forecast for Year 2	£
Cash in	
Sales	500,000
Cash out	
Raw materials	250,000
Selling expenses	120,000
Distribution expenses	30,000
Administration expenses	20,000
Purchase of production facility	150,000
Additional working capital	60,000
	630,000
Net cash inflow/(outflow)	(130,000)

Table 4.12 *Squishies Ltd: capital investment proposal Year 2 – France*

This forecast shows that by using the existing production facility, and with high expenditure on advertising, a rapid growth in sales can be achieved whilst phasing in the Squishies brand. It will cost £150,000 to purchase the production facility and it is estimated that an additional £60,000 will be tied up at any one time in stocks and debtors.

Overall, the statement shows an outflow of £130,000. As seen in other sections, an outflow in the first year of a new venture is almost inevitable and on the face of it the figures look promising.

Forecast profit and balance sheet

If we presume no change in the UK figures for Year 2, we can put these cash flow figures together with the Year 1 figures for the UK to get the preliminary forecast for Year 2 as shown in Table 4.13.

(N.B. *you may spot that depreciation adjustments have been ignored in preparing these figures. This is because they would increase the complexity of the numbers without changing the message the statements contain for management.*)

Trace through the origin of all the numbers in the profit and loss account and balance sheet. The profit and loss account, fixed assets and working capital figures are simply arrived at by adding the UK Year 1 figures to the Year 2 forecast cash flow figures for the French operation. Shareholders' funds are the balance of £100,000 at the end of Year 1 plus the Year 2 profit of £200,000. Treat the £410,000 for borrowings as a balancing figure – it is whatever number is needed to make both sides of the balance sheet equal £710,000.

Profit and loss account forecast for Year 2	£	Balance sheet as at 31 December, Year 2	£
Sales	1,300,000	Fixed assets	450,000
Cost of sales	600,000		
		Working capital	260,000
Gross profit	700,000		710,000
Expenses			
Selling expenses	340,000		
Distribution	80,000		
Administration	80,000		
	500,000		
Net profit	200,000	Funded by	
		Shareholders' funds	300,000
		Borrowings	410,000
			710,000
Return on capital employed	28%		
Net profit margin	15%		
Asset turnover (times)	1.83		

Table 4.13 *Squishies Ltd: preliminary forecast for Year 2*

Looking at the figures, going ahead with the French venture will increase profits from £120,000 to £200,000. ROCE will also increase because although the net profit margin stays the same at 15 per cent, the assets are used more efficiently, with an increase in asset turnover to 1.83.

From the numbers, this appears to be a very attractive way to grow the company whilst maintaining profitability and increasing the return made on the capital employed in the business.

Evaluating the financial forecasts

Imagine you have been called in by the CEO as an independent advisor to carry out a critical evaluation of the French proposal. Some of the main areas of concern that you might raise with the management team that are championing the proposal are as follows:

◆ The sales for the French operation in the first year represent over 60 per cent of current UK sales. This is a very major expansion of the business.

◆ Why is the existing owner selling? Is it because its own sales are declining? Are we being overoptimistic about both the speed with which we can introduce Squishies in France and the investment in marketing needed?

◆ What is the age and quality of the production facilities we will be purchasing and are we familiar with the technology?

◆ What are the relationships with the distributors?

Imagine that the project goes ahead, and that as the British managers get to know their French counterparts better they are optimistic about the long-term success of the business and they feel that the decision to go ahead was the right one. However, there have been more problems than had been anticipated and everything is taking considerably longer than expected. In particular, they have had to replace the major distributors, meaning that sales for the current year will only be a fraction of what was originally hoped.

In the light of these changed circumstances, management produces a revised cash flow forecast for Year 2, as shown in Table 4.14.

Revised cash flow forecast for Year 2	£
Cash in	
Sales	100,000
Cash out	
Raw materials	70,000
Selling expenses	40,000
Distribution expenses	20,000
Administration expenses	10,000
Purchase of production facility	150,000
Additional working capital	30,000
	320,000
Net cash inflow/(outflow)	220,000

Table 4.14 *Squishies Ltd: capital invesment proposal Year 2 – France*

Whilst forecast sales are dramatically lower for Year 2, the company has still had to make the expenditure necessary for the long-term success of the acquisition. The revised forecast shows a cash outflow for the year of £220,000.

What effect does all this have on the company's forecast profit and loss account and balance sheet? The revised forecasts are shown in Table 4.15.

Profit and loss account forecast for Year 2	£	Balance sheet as at 31 December, Year 2	£
Sales	900,000	Fixed assets	450,000
Cost of sales	420,000		
Gross profit	480,000	Working capital	230,000
			680,000
Expenses			
		Funded by	
Selling expenses	260,000	Shareholders' funds	180,000
Distribution	70,000	Borrowings	500,000
Administration	70,000		
	400,000		680,000
Net profit	80,000		
Return on capital employed	12%		
Net profit margin	9%		
Asset turnover (times)	1.32		

Table 4.15 *Squishies Ltd: revised forcast for Year 2*

The answer is that it has a pretty disastrous effect on the results of the company for Year 2:

- ◆ Net profit has dropped from £120,000 to £80,000
- ◆ Return on capital employed has halved from 24 per cent to 12 per cent, caused by deterioration in both the net profit margin and asset turnover ratios
- ◆ Borrowings have increased by 25 per cent to £500,000.

These figures will require careful selling to the shareholders in the company. The medium to long-term prospects may be good but the company will need to show how it intends to turn the French operation round.

Note too that management is now severely constrained in terms of taking advantage of other investment opportunities. If it needs to make investment in the UK to defend its market share, or if an excellent opportunity arises to invest in another country, it will have great difficulty in raising the necessary funds. This is for two reasons:

- Its ratio of borrowings to shareholders' funds at 280 per cent (500,000 ÷ 180,000 × 100) is already high.

- The track record of the company's management is now suspect. When investors look for investment opportunities, the perceived quality of the management team is everything.

This concludes our introduction to capital investment decisions. The situation becomes more complicated where an organisation is planning a number of years ahead, with irregular cash flows in each of the projected years. Here one must recognise that an organisation will value future cash flows less highly the further into the future they take place.

Controlling working capital

In order to maximise our return on capital employed (ROCE) we need to maximise our profit margin and the utilisation of our assets. In this section you explore the investment made in the working capital employed in the business.

Components of working capital

Look again at the financial statement of Squishies Ltd, shown in Table 4.16.

Profit and loss account for Year 1	£	Balance sheet as at 31 December, Year 1	£
Sales	800,000	Fixed assets	300,000
Cost of sales	350,000		
		Working capital	
Gross profit	450,000	Stock	80,000
		Debtors	140,000
Expenses		Bank	30,000
		Less: Creditors	(50,000)
Selling expenses	220,000		
Distribution	50,000		200,000
Administration	60,000		
	330,000		500,000
Net profit	120,000	Funded by	
		Shareholders' funds	100,000
		Borrowings	400,000
			500,000
Return on capital employed	24%		
Net profit margin	15%		
Asset turnover (times)	1.60		

Table 4.16 *Squishies Ltd: financial statement, Year 1*

We see that Squishies has an investment of £200,000 in working capital. You will also see these headings referred to as current assets – the terms are used interchangeably.

Remember that the balance sheet is drawn up at a particular point in time. The different balance sheet headings show the value of the assets and liabilities at that point in time.

See the earlier section in this book, 'Making assets work harder', for a description of balance sheet headings.

As a reminder, the headings are as follows:

Stock
This represents the value of all the raw materials, work-in-progress and finished goods.

Debtors
This is the total amount owed to us by our customers, or to put it another way, all sales invoices unpaid at the balance sheet date.

Bank
This is simply the amount of money we have in the bank, or if we have gone into the red, the amount of money we owe the bank.

Creditors
The mirror image of debtors – this represents the total amount we owe our suppliers at the balance sheet date.

Squishies is a manufacturing company but all types of businesses will have working capital. A firm of accountants may have considerable sums of money tied up in work-in-progress – work it has carried out for clients but not yet billed. Construction companies have long lead times and will need to make sure they have the funding in place to finance their work-in-progress. Retail outlets may have no debtors because they sell for cash but they must hold stock, which they can finance partly through the credit extended to them by suppliers.

Working capital and cash flow management

You may not be familiar with thinking of the money tied up in these items as 'investments', using that term instead for long-term investments. Some of the money tied up in working capital may vary due to, say, seasonal demand. However, there will be a certain amount of funds permanently tied up in working capital and it is perfectly right to say that this is an investment.

To put this another way:

> ◆ All companies exist to add value to what they buy in – be it raw materials, people or information. To purchase what they need they must pay their suppliers and their workforce. Mostly they will get credit from their suppliers and pay their workforce in arrears.
>
> ◆ On a day-to-day basis, the company's only source of income is the money it receives and banks from its customers.
>
> ◆ Generally, companies have to pay their suppliers before they get the money from their customers. This causes what is known as a trading funding gap and it is this gap that must be funded and represents an investment by the company.

Like any assets, this investment must be funded either from shareholders or by borrowings. The more money we have tied up in working capital, the less money we will have available for investment in the long-term assets that are essential for the company's growth and survival.

The control of working capital

Minimising our investment in working capital is all about *time*. The quicker we move stocks through the premises and the faster we can get customers to pay, the less money we will have tied up in working capital.

The starting point for any management action is to relate the main types of current assets to the reasons we have to make the investment at all.

To take debtors first. We have debtors because we make sales to customers. The more sales we make to our customers the higher the debtors figure we can expect to have. From a control point of view, what interests us is how long on average our customers are taking to pay. This is commonly referred to as the number of days debtors. The figures for Squishies are:

Average daily sales: £800,000 ÷ 365   =   *£2,192*
Debtors at 31 December Year 1   =   *£140,000*
Number of days debtors: £140,000 ÷ £2,192   =   *64 days*

So we can say that our customers are paying us, on average, after 64 days.

Is this good or bad? Well, it depends. If your standard terms are 30 days, then it is poor. If, however, you operate in an industry where all your competitors give 90 days credit, then you are doing well.

Creditors are, as usual, the mirror image of debtors. Here it is purchases that give rise to creditors – if we did not buy things then we would not owe our suppliers anything. We do not have the figure for purchases and so will use the figure for cost of sales from the profit and loss account as an approximation in order to calculate days creditors:

> *Average daily cost of sales: £350,000 ÷ 365*   =   *£959*
> *Creditors at 31 December Year 1*   =   *£50,000*
> *Number of days creditors: £50,000 ÷ £959*   =   *52 days*

So we are obtaining, on average, 52 days credit from our suppliers. As this credit is a form of interest-free funding for the business, we want to take as many days as possible. We must be careful, however, that we maintain good relationships with our suppliers. If we persist in taking too long to pay, they may quietly increase their prices to us to compensate.

Finally, we hold stock in order to manufacture goods. Alternatively, if we provide a service, we may have money tied up in work-in-progress representing work carried out for clients which we have yet to bill. We will relate stocks to the cost of sales figure, hence:

> *Average daily cost of sales: £350,000 ÷ 365*   =   *£959*
> *Stock at 31 December Year 1*   =   *£80,000*
> *Number of days stock: £80,000 ÷ £959*   =   *83 days*

We can therefore say that stock is equal to 83 days of cost of sales or production. As with debtors and creditors, this figure could be compared with last year or budget to see whether we are improving. Companies could also benchmark – investigate the same ratios in other companies, perhaps their leading competitors, to see how they are performing against industry standards.

Activity 14
Analysing utilisation of assets

Objectives

This activity builds upon the analysis of Wheetman plc's accounts which was started in Activity 12 and continued in Activity 13.

In this activity you will complete your analysis of Wheetman plc by investigating how efficiently it is using its assets together with the related question of cash flow.

Use this activity to:

◆ compare the current profit performance of a company using comparative data

◆ produce key asset usage ratios and analysis

◆ evaluate the financial results.

The balance sheet for Wheetman plc is reproduced in Table 4.17.

	2001 £000	2000 £000
Fixed assets	8,235	4,300
Current assets		
Stocks	2,410	1,209
Trade debtors	1,372	807
Other debtors	201	134
Cash	4	28
	3,987	2,178
Current liabilities		
Trade creditors	1,306	607
Other creditors	201	124
Taxation	390	210
Dividends	400	300
Overdraft	1,625	–
	(3,922)	(1,241)
Net current assets	65	937
Total net assets	8,300	5,237
Bank loan	3,800	1,800
	4,500	3,437
Share capital	1,800	1,800
Capital reserve	952	952
Retained profits	1,748	685
	4,500	3,437

Table 4.17 *Wheetman plc: balance sheet as at 31 March 2001*

Task

1 Produce figures for:

Number of days stock

Number of days debtors (use only trade debtors)

Number of days creditors (use only trade creditors)

2 Then consider how the cash and borrowings position has changed between the two years. Review the ratios you have just produced and compare the balance sheet for the two years to determine the main reasons for the change in the cash and borrowing position.

3 Draw up a list of questions to ask local management.

The cash and borrowing position:

Questions for local management:

Feedback

The company's cash position has deteriorated greatly during 2001. Borrowings from the bank have increased from £1.8 million to £3.8 million and the company is operating on a new overdraft facility of £1.6 million. Total borrowings have therefore increased by £3.6 million. Against shareholders' funds totalling £4.5 million, this is a major increase.

What has caused this state of affairs? The major reason is that fixed assets have increased from £4.3 million to more than £8.2 million. We know that Wheetman plc has introduced a new product range and that sales have subsequently increased by 60 per cent. We might ask:

◆ Was the 2001 major capital expenditure programme undertaken as planned or were there overspends?

◆ In terms of the company's overall strategy, have the anticipated benefits from this expenditure been realised and are the projections for future years still in line with original planning?

◆ Turning from fixed assets to working capital, we can look at the three ratios you calculated – see Table 4.18.

		2001	2000
Number of days stock	Stock ÷ (Cost of sales ÷ 365)	2,410 ÷ (5,809 ÷ 365) = 151	1,209 ÷ (3,748 ÷ 365) = 117
Number of days debtors	Trade debtors ÷ (Sales ÷ 365)	1,372 ÷ (11,205 ÷ 365) = 45	807 ÷ (7,003 ÷ 365) = 42
Number of days creditors	Trade creditors ÷ (Cost of sales ÷ 365)	1,306 ÷ (5,809 ÷ 365) = 82	607 ÷ (3,748 ÷ 365) = 59

Table 4.18 *Calculation of ratios*

The situation with stock turnover has deteriorated badly, with stock now equal to 151 days of production costs against a 2000 figure of 117 days. This is particularly serious in terms of cash flow as the stock figure would have risen with the increase in sales even if last year's ratio had been maintained. We need to know:

◆ Why have the number of days of stock deteriorated?

◆ Has management been so busy chasing sales and overseeing capital investment projects that it has taken its eye off the ball in terms of day-to-day stock control?

Trade debtors are more or less unchanged at 45 days and so this probably need not be regarded as an area for us to investigate at the moment as there are more important variances.

The company is taking more credit from its suppliers, paying them on average in 82 days as compared to 49 days in 2000. We might ask:

◆ Is this longer payment period affecting the relationship with the company's suppliers? Is management sure its suppliers are not increasing prices to the company in order to compensate for the increased credit terms?

This concludes our financial review of Wheetman plc. This review has enabled us to pick out the key changes in the financial performance of the company. It is now up to local management to provide credible answers to those questions and present their plans for the company's future success.

Funding the business

Sources of finance

If you acquire a new car, you become the proud owner of a new asset: the car. You will be only too aware that the acquisition of the car must be funded in some way – either out of savings or by borrowing the money. The actual purchase may be made out of your bank account, but you have to ensure there are sufficient funds in your account at the time of purchase.

Similarly for a business, if the assets employed in a business increase then that increase in assets must be funded in some way. As with the individual, a company has choices about how to fund the acquisition of assets. Over time the business has the choice between:

- ◆ retaining the profits it has made in the business rather than paying them out to shareholders
- ◆ going to its shareholders and asking them to put more money into the business
- ◆ borrowing from the bank or issuing debentures.

Let us take each of these three methods, using an example to illustrate the options open to a company. The financial statement of Miah Enterprises plc, for the end of a year which we will call Year X, is shown in Table 4.19.

Profit and loss account year ended 31 December Year X	£
Sales	1,500,000
Expenses	1,120,000
Operating profit	380,000
Interest	35,000
Profit before taxation	345,000
Taxation	120,000
Profit after taxation	225,000
Dividends	95,000
Retained profit	130,000

Market value of £1 share at 31 December Year X was £34

Balance sheet as at 31 December Year X	£
Fixed assets	500,000
Working capital	
Stock	60,000
Debtors	120,000
Bank	50,000
	230,000
(Creditors)	40,000
	190,000
	690,000
Funded by	
Shareholders' funds	
Ordinary £1 shares	80,000
Opening reserves	200,000
Retained profit for year	130,000
Closing reserves	330,000
Total shareholders' funds	410,000
Borrowings	280,000
	690,000

Table 4.19 *Miah Enterprises plc: financial statement*

The left-hand side of Table 4.19 shows the profit and loss account for Miah Enterprises for the year to 31 December Year X. There are two headings for payments made to the providers of funding for the business: the company has paid £35,000 in interest on its borrowings and £95,000 to its shareholders by way of dividends. In addition, the company owes the government £120,000 in tax on the profits it has made.

On the right-hand side of Table 4.19 is the balance sheet for Miah Enterprises at the end of Year X. It shows that Miah has £690,000 worth of assets employed in the business. These assets will have been acquired over time – in the case of the fixed assets, over many years. The balance sheet gives a snapshot of the assets at a single point in time.

The balance sheet shows that the shareholders have funded £410,000 worth of the assets with the remaining £280,000 funded by borrowing.

Shareholders' funds

A company is owned by its shareholders. The directors of a company are appointed by the shareholders and are legally responsible to them; they act as the agents of the shareholders in the running of the company.

Let us say that Miah Enterprises was set up in 1990. To start the company, 80,000 £1 ordinary shares were issued to a group of investors. The investors paid £1 for each share and so the company was able to bank £80,000 from the issue of the shares. This is clearly a source of funding for the business.

When we talk of £1 ordinary shares, the '£1' is only the **nominal value**. In the case of Miah, each £1 share entitles the person holding that share to 1/80,000 of the value of the whole company. So, for example, an institution holding 10,000 shares would own an eighth of the company. In public companies shares can be traded and in the case of Miah, Table 4.19 tells us that one £1 share had a market value of £34 at the end of Year X.

> We can see that shareholders take their rewards in two ways:
> ◆ by the receipt of dividends paid out of profits
> ◆ by the increase in the market value of the shares they hold, known as **capital growth**.

As so often in life, the shareholders cannot have it both ways – the more shareholders take out of a business through the payment of dividends, the less is left in the company to fund growth.

In the case of Miah, £95,000 has been paid out as dividends, leaving £130,000 retained in the business. This retained profit is a source of funding for the business – in fact it is the major source of funding for most companies.

Shareholders' funds, also known as **equity**, are thus made up of money received from share issues plus any profits retained in the business. This is also known as the **risk capital** because there is no legal obligation on the company to pay a dividend and the shareholders' fortunes rise and fall with the fortunes of the company.

Borrowings

Like individuals, companies can go out and borrow to fund their activities. The lenders of the money receive their reward in the form of interest – they receive an agreed percentage of what has been borrowed each year. The interest rate will be agreed at the time the loan is taken out and the company is contractually obligated to pay it whatever its financial circumstances. Thus the lenders do not share in the fortunes of the company in the same way as the shareholders.

Again, unlike the shareholders, the banks or other institutions will expect to receive back the original sum, the **capital**, lent to the company. The repayment terms will be part of the original contract between the company and the lender.

Borrowings can take several forms and these are summarised in Table 4.20.

Bank overdraft	A facility agreed with the bank whereby the company can borrow up to an agreed limit. The advantage is that the company only pays interest on what it needs to borrow on a daily basis. The disadvantages are that this type of borrowing is usually expensive and that the facility can be withdrawn at any time.
Loans	Loans are usually made by banks but can be provided by other institutions such as pension funds. The terms of the loan include covenants designed to protect the interests of the lender, for example, it may limit the ability of the company to take out further loans. To further protect the lender in the case of liquidation of the company, the loan may be secured either on all the company's assets or on specific assets.
Debentures (also known as bonds or loan stock)	These are loans issued in the form of securities so that they can be traded in the same way as shares. Hence a loan of £1 million may be divided into £100 units, each of which can be bought and sold on the stock exchange. The value of each unit will vary according to general interest rates and any perceived risk of non repayment.
Finance leasing	This is used to fund the purchase of specific assets. Here the financial institution buys the asset on behalf of the company and leases it in return for a regular payment for an agreed period.

Table 4.20 *Forms of borrowing*

Not all forms of funding fall neatly into the categories of equity or borrowing. For example, convertible loan stock is a type of debenture where the lender has the option to convert the amount lent into shares in the company at a predetermined price. Thus if the company does well, the lender can participate in that success by buying shares at below the current market price.

Gearing and leverage

It is part of the duties of the directors of a company to decide how much of the business to fund by equity and how much by borrowings – **the funding decision**.

The most attractive option might appear to be simply to stop paying dividends and retain all the profits in the business. Compared with paying a dividend and then taking out a loan, this appears to be 'free' funding because the company must pay interest on loans but has no obligation to pay dividends.

In reality, retained profits are not free. The company's shareholders require an income stream as a reward for investing in the company and if they do not receive it, will stop buying the company's shares. The fall in market share price will make it difficult or impossible for the company to raise money by issuing new shares when it needs to.

In fact, equity finance is generally more expensive than borrowings because the shareholders carry more risk. Interest payments must be made before any dividends are declared and in the event of a company being liquidated, shareholders are the last to be paid out of any remaining assets. In addition, interest payments are allowed as a deduction when calculating profit for taxation purposes whilst no such deduction can be made for dividends.

If borrowings are cheaper, then what is to constrain the company from always relying on borrowing for additional funding? The constraint is that there is a greater risk associated with borrowing because, unlike dividends, the interest payments must be made whatever the current trading conditions.

The ratio between debt and equity is known as the **gearing** or **debt/equity** ratio. If a company has a high ratio of debt to equity it is said to be highly leveraged. In highly leveraged companies, shareholders have higher gains during the good times but run a higher risk during a recession that profits will be insufficient to meet interest payments.

There is no right or wrong gearing ratio for a company. Companies should compare their ratios with those for other companies in their industry. Also, over time the relative costs of debt and equity finance will alter and the funding decision needs to be made in the light of current conditions in the financial markets.

◆ Recap

Explore techniques for monitoring trends in financial performance

◆ Restating the figures in financial reports as percentages makes it easier to identify trends in performance and carry out 'what-if' analyses. Common size analysis is an example where the figures from the profit and loss statement are presented as a percentage of sales.

◆ Indicators like the gross profit margin, the gross profit (sales less the cost of good bought in) expressed as a percentage of sales, are similarly useful.

◆ Variance analysis (the difference between forecast and budget costs) is a more valuable technique for monitoring movement in individual overheads because it considers overheads in isolation from the impact of sales.

Find out how to analyse the profitability of an organisation using the major profitability ratios

◆ The major ratios used to measure how well a business generates profit are:

- return on capital employed (ROCE)

- asset turnover

- net profit margin.

- ROCE measures the percentage return a company is earning on the money invested in it. Ideally, a company's ROCE should be increasing year on year as it makes better use of its assets.

Describe what is meant by capital investment and appraise the financial statement supporting an investment proposal

- Large, long-term purchases or expenses, such as premises, start-up costs, machinery and other fixed assets, are generally paid for by investment capital.

Discover the components of and main ways of controlling working capital

- Working capital is the money used to finance short-term expenses, such as customer credit, saleable goods or materials, stock and wages. A business should aim to minimise its working capital.

- Three key measures indicate how effectively a company is controlling its working capital: number of debtor days, number of creditor days and number of days stock.

Distinguish between the three main sources of finance for a business and explore what is meant by gearing

- The main sources of finance for an organisation are retained profits, borrowings or through issuing shares.

- Gearing is concerned with the long-term ability of the business to service its long-term debt. The gearing ratio measures the proportion of **debt** to **equity**.

▶▶ **More @**

Broadbent, M. and Cullen, J. (2003) *Managing Financial Resources*, Butterworth-Heinemann

Owen, A. (2003) *Accounting for Business Studies*, Butterworth-Heinemann

The above texts are designed for managers who want to develop their financial management capabilities further – they cover similar ground to this book, but in greater depth.

Bized is an award-winning site providing learning resources on business and economics related subjects. For a direct link to pages on profitability analysis, try **http://www.bized.ac.uk/compfact/ratios/index.htm**

McKenzie, W. (2003) *FT Guide to Using and Interpreting Company Accounts*, **Financial Times Prentice Hall**
Part 2 of this wide-ranging text takes you through analysing a set of company accounts from an investor's perspective to make an assessment of a business's solvency and profitability.

Harvey, D., McLaney, E. and Atrill, P. (2001), *Accounting for Business*, **Butterworth-Heinemann**
This book provides a detailed analysis of the key financial statements, and how to compile and analyse them.

5 External reporting

Companies are legal entities which are required by law to publish their financial accounts. Increasingly, organisations in the public and not-for-profit sectors are also required to publish similar accounts to report on their financial performance during the year. This theme describes some of the requirements and issues around the publication of financial information for public consumption.

In this theme you will:

◆ **Consider the requirement to publish financial accounts**

◆ **Identify the key issues in the preparation of financial information**

◆ **Consider the international dimension to financial reporting.**

External reporting

This theme describes UK external reporting requirements but there are substantial similarities across all the advanced economies. The theme ends with a consideration of international reporting requirements.

Published accounts

In a limited liability company, the shareholders' potential loss is limited to the value of the shares held in the company. This contrasts with a sole trader or a partnership where the creditors of the business can pursue the owners for their private assets. All limited liability companies are required to publish accounts so that the creditors and other trading partners of the company can assess its creditworthiness.

A limited liability company that offers its shares to the public is known as a **public company**, and a whole further set of reporting requirements must be met before the shares can be actively bought and sold. In the UK, the stock exchange is where this trading in shares takes place. Having shares traded on the stock exchange is attractive to:

◆ shareholders because they can liquidate their investment in a particular company at any time

◆ companies because they can raise substantial sums of money, both directly through the issues of shares and by the issue of loan stock.

For all advanced economies, the existence of a stock exchange, by whatever name, is essential to provide a market where financial securities (shares and loan stock) can be traded and new capital raised. To operate efficiently, the financial markets require information, and the extensive reporting requirements placed on companies are designed to meet this need.

In the UK, each public company is required to produce an annual report which sets out a wealth of detail on its operations and financial results for the year. The content of the annual report is laid down by company law and the stock exchange, with additional requirements made by the major professional accounting bodies.

Auditing and accounting standards

It is not enough that companies report all the required financial information in their annual reports; investors need to have confidence that the information is reliable and can be safely compared with that for other companies.

The legal duty to prepare the accounts of a company rests firmly with its directors. In addition, the law requires that the accounts are audited by a recognised professional firm of accountants who then report on whether the accounts show a true and fair view of the affairs of the company.

Because there are so many subjective areas in the preparation of accounts, it is of little value to ask whether accounts are 'accurate' or 'correct'. All one can hope to do is to prepare the accounts according to established accounting principles and then report on any difficult areas.

This degree of subjectivity in the preparation of accounts comes as a surprise to many people but consider these three brief examples, all of which are similar to stories that appear in the financial press from time to time.

Stock valuation
A PC (personal computer) manufacturer is holding a high value of stock at its year-end. There is talk of the launch of new technology by a major competitor which could force the manufacturer to sell its PCs at below cost. *Should the company continue to value its stock at cost or should it write the stock down and report lower profits?*

Fixed assets
A company has made a major investment in telecommunications networks. There is now overcapacity in the industry, with little hope of the company ever making enough profits to recover its investment. *How should the company value its investment in the telecommunications networks?*

> **Recognition of income**
> Trading during the year has been poor, but towards the year-end a company signs an important three-year contract with a new customer. It is estimated that the contract will yield profits of £1 million over the three years. *How much profit from the contract should the company show in this year's accounts?*

For each example, the answer to the question will depend upon the view taken by the company and its auditors. In an attempt to reduce the amount of discretion companies have in reporting their results, the accounting bodies lay down accounting standards which must be followed in the preparation of company accounts. These standards are continuously evolving over time and cover all the areas where there is most likely to be disagreement, such as stock valuation, research and development, depreciation and pensions.

International reporting

The globalisation of commerce is continuing to have a profound effect on the need for financial information and the way it is reported. Multinational companies require standardisation of financial reporting across all the countries in which they operate. The capital markets that provide the funds for companies now operate around the clock through the major financial centres across the world. The tremendous growth in cross-border mergers and acquisitions over the last 10 years has created its own pressures for international standardisation.

In the UK, company legislation already follows that laid down by the European Union. The UK was also a founder member of the International Accounting Standards Committee (IASC) which was formed in 1973. The aim of the IASC is to make financial statements more comparable on a worldwide basis and to date over 40 international accounting standards have been issued. Rather than develop their own accounting standards, many countries are adopting these international accounting standards as their own requirements.

There is still a long way to go, however. In the USA, companies wishing for a listing on the New York Stock Exchange must still prepare accounts in accordance with US Generally Accepted Accounting Principles (GAAP) in addition to the requirements of their home country. Thus a multinational company may have to produce a number of sets of accounts, for example:

◆ financial statements to meet the requirements of its home country

◆ financial accounts to meet the requirements of other countries in which its shares are quoted or in which it raises capital

◆ adjusted accounts in every country in which it operates to meet local company law and taxation requirements.

Activity 15
Published accounts – the profit and loss account

Objectives

This activity centres on the published profit and loss account. Use this activity to:

◆ describe the headings in a published profit and loss account

◆ review the published profit and loss account for your organisation

◆ evaluate the profit performance for your organisation.

Task

Set out as an example, Table 5.1 is the profit and loss account for Yate Brothers Wine Lodges plc, a UK wine bar operator.

	£000
Turnover	144,049
Net operating costs	(125,041)
Operating profit	19,008
Share of profits of associates	390
Exceptional items	(710)
Profit on ordinary activities before interest	18,688
Net interest payable	(3,818)
Profit on ordinary activities before tax	14,870
Taxation	(1,885)
Profit for the financial year	12,985
Dividends	(3,219)
Retained profit	9,766

Table 5.1 *Yate Brothers Wine Lodges plc: profit and loss account*

Many of the headings in Table 5.1 have been explained in earlier themes and in other activities, but we will recap here – see Table 5.2.

Turnover	This is another word for sales. See our earlier sections on cash and profit for a definition and an explanation of the difference between cash inflow and sales
Net operating costs	These include all the costs of the company excluding interest and taxation. They therefore include the cost of sales and overheads
Share of profits of associates	This is Yate's share of the profits of a company in which it has a substantial shareholding but which it does not actually own
Exceptional items	Included here are one-off income and expenses which fall outside the normal trading activities of the business – in Yate's case they relate to losses on property transactions
Net interest payable	This is the interest payable on loans less interest received on deposits. See our earlier section on funding the business for an explanation of interest
Taxation	This is tax payable to the government on the profits generated by the business
Dividends	These are payable to the company's shareholders. For a discussion of dividends, consult the section on funding the business

Table 5.2 *Profit and loss account headings*

This leaves the retained profit which will be used by the company to maintain and grow the business.

Task

Obtain a copy of the latest annual published accounts for your organisation and then do the following:

1 Compare the profit and loss account headings with those in the example given in this activity.

2 Obtain explanations for any further headings used. Note your findings below.

3 Using the techniques set out in the section on reviewing financial performance, review the profitability of your organisation.

Profit and loss account headings compared:

Explanations for further headings used:

Review of the profitability of your organisation

Feedback

The reporting requirements for public companies set out a large volume of financial data and analysis which must be included in the annual accounts. In reviewing your own organisation's profit and loss account you will probably discover much additional information disclosed by way of notes to the main financial statement.

Much of this information is aimed at investment analysts and it is not necessary for you to understand the derivation of all the numbers. Try to gain explanations from your finance department of the main figures in the report.

Once you have carried out your common size analysis and the other techniques outlined earlier, write down four or five key points about your organisation's performance for the year.

Finally, look up press reports on results for the year you are analysing and compare your analysis of the profit and loss account with the comments in the financial press. Your public relations department or similar will have copies of press commentary on your organisation. You can also find sites on the Internet which will provide additional analysis.

Activity 16
Published accounts – the balance sheet

Objectives

The purpose of this activity is to review the published balance sheet of an organisation.

Use this activity to:

◆ describe the headings on a published balance sheet

◆ review the published balance sheet for your organisation

◆ evaluate the press comment on the financial results for your organisation.

The example balance sheet shown in Table 5.3 is taken from the annual accounts of Yate Brothers Wine Lodges plc, a UK operator of a chain of wine bars.

	£000
Fixed assets	
Tangible	192,215
Investments	3,903
	196,118
Current assets	
Stocks	4,284
Debtors	9,815
Cash at bank and in hand	5,212
	19,311
Creditors due within one year	(30,617)
Net current liabilities	(11,306)
Total assets less current liabilities	184,812
Creditors due after one year	(75,503)
Provision for liabilities and charges	(1,794)
	107,515
Capital and reserves	
Share capital	16,209
Reserves	91,306
Shareholder's funds	107,515

Table 5.3 *Yate Brothers Wine Lodges plc: balance sheet*

The meanings of the various headings are set out in Table 5.4.

Fixed assets: tangible	These are assets bought for long-term use within the business which are physically present, for example, premises and bar equipment. Occasionally organisations will show intangible assets on their balance sheets – an example would be the value of a patent held by a company
Fixed assets: investments	This is the value of the long-term investments Yates has made in other companies
Stocks	For Yates this would be the value of the wine, beer, food, etc. held on the premises at the year-end
Debtors	These are amounts owed to the organisation by its customers and any advances made to its trading partners. Included here will also be any payments made in advance; in the case of Yates this would include rent on some of its wine bars
Cash at bank and in hand	This is cash in the tills and in the bank
Creditors due within one year	Included here are bank overdraft facilities, trade creditors, tax payable, accruals and the proposed dividend
Creditors due after one year	This is comprised of the bank loans made to the organisation
Provisions for liabilities and charges	These are technical adjustments for tax allowances repayable should the activities of the organisation be wound down
Share capital	This is the nominal value of shares issued by the company
Reserves	These are mainly the profits retained by the business

Table 5.4 *Balance sheet headings*

Task

Obtain a copy of the latest annual published accounts for your organisation and then:

1 Compare the balance sheet headings with those in the example given in this activity.

2 Obtain explanations for any further headings used.

3 Obtain press reports on the financial results set out in the published accounts.

Balance sheet headings compared:

Explanations for further headings used:

Press reports on financial results:

Feedback

You will find several pages of notes to the accounts, setting out more detailed information on each of the balance sheet headings. Much of this information is only of interest to specialist investment analysts but read through it and ask about anything you do not understand.

Again, ask your public relations department or similar for copies of press commentary on your organisation and search for sites on the Internet which provide additional analysis.

Read through the commentary and trace any references to specific figures back to the accounts. Make sure you understand the press commentary and reflect upon whether you agree with what is being said about the organisation you work for. If there is anything you do not understand, now is an excellent opportunity to ask your manager or finance department for an explanation.

◆ Recap

Consider the requirement to publish financial accounts

◆ Limited liability companies are required to publish accounts so that stakeholders can assess their creditworthiness.

◆ Public limited companies are also required to publish annual reports which provide additional detail on operations and financial results.

Identify the key issues in the preparation of financial information

◆ The law requires that companies prepare their accounts in accordance with UK accounting standards and have them audited by an accountant.

◆ These standards are continually evolving but there is still an element of discretion in the preparation of accounts.

Consider the international dimension to financial reporting

◆ A multinational company may need to prepare several sets of accounts to meet the requirements of countries in which it trades shares and/or operates.

◆ The International Accounting Standards Committee, of which the UK is a member, aims to make financial statements comparable on a worldwide basis.

 **More @**

Harvey, D., McLaney, E. and Atrill, P. (2001), *Accounting for Business*, Butterworth-Heinemann
This book focuses on financial accounting as opposed to financial management. Aimed primarily at accounting students, it provides a detailed analysis of the accounting framework and requirements for external reporting.

For more information on US accounting conventions, see **www.accountingstudy.com**

Annual reports Service – http://annualreports.money.msn.co.uk
This site provides annual reports for a selected range of companies free of charge. It also provides advice on reading reports.

References

Attril, P. and McLaney, E. A. (2000) 3rd edition, *Accounting and finance for non-specialists,* Financial Times

Broadbent, M. and Cullen, J. (2003) 3rd edition, *Managing Financial Resources,* Butterworth-Heinemann

Grundy, T with Johnson, G. and Scholes K. (1998) 1st edition, *Exploring strategic financial management,* Prentice Hall Europe

Owen, A. (2003) *Accounting for Business Studies,* Butterworth-Heinemann